Lead Your Journey:

Decide to be the CEO of Your Life

Lead Your Journey:

Decide to be the CEO of Your Life

Doug Packard

Published by Packard Publishing

Copyright @2017 by Douglas Packard

All rights reserved. This book or any portion thereof may not be reproduced or used in any manner whatsoever without the express written permission of the publisher except for the use of brief quotations in a book review.

Printed in the United States of America

First Printing, 2017

ISBN 978-0-692-88464-5

Lead Your Journey: Decide to be the CEO of Your Life
Written by Doug Packard
Edited by Jeff Pike
Cover designed by Kim Traina

First published in the United States in 2017 by:
Packard Publishing
Portland, Maine

www.DougPackardConsulting.com

Acknowledgements

To my writing partner Jeff Pike. I could not have accomplished this book without your encouragement, skills, and friendship.

To my long-time associate and friend Judi Jones for managing the technical details.

To creative expert Kim Traina for the cover design.

To my wife and family for their support, love, and patience.

To my parents for always believing in me and challenging me to stretch toward my dreams.

To my clients from whom I have learned so much. I am deeply grateful that you have allowed me to be a part of your journey.

Jeff Pike is a freelance writer who ghost-writes books for business leaders and helps businesses communicate their expertise and their customer success. He can be contacted at jeffpike@bwservices.net. For more information, visit www.bwservices.net.

In her business, Jumpstart Creative, Kim Traina, helps businesses communicate, educate and enlighten with design, photography and marketing strategies.
Kim can be reached at hello@calljumpstart.com.

Table of Contents

Introduction: Live Your Life—The Way You Are Meant To vii

Chapter 1: Build Relationships—with Yourself and Others 1

Chapter 2: Self-Management 13

Chapter 3: Set Goals to Plan for Success 25

Chapter 4: Manage Your Energy and Your Focus 33

Chapter 5: Maximize Your Return-On-Time 43

Chapter 6: Change Your Environments 55

Chapter 7: Manage Your Attitude Towards Money 67

Chapter 8: Putting It All Together 79

Introduction: Live Your Life—The Way You Are Meant To

Thanks for taking a look at my very first, and maybe only, book! As a business coach since 2002, I've learned a lot from the many leaders I've had the privilege to collaborate with—as I have assisted them with their journeys to improve both their business and their personal lives. It's a journey I often refer to as making a transition from living your life the way you are "supposed to" towards living your life the way you are "meant to."

I hope this book helps you on your journey.

For me, the major transformation took place after working more than 20 years in the corporate world after I had steadily progressed from functional positions to strategic roles. I earned a very good living and achieved my financial and executive identity objectives. Although I was not completely fulfilled, I was quite comfortable and had resigned myself to the benefits of the situation I was in.

I also avoided answering the question of what I was truly "meant to do" and thus suppressed my feelings. Instead, I focused on what I was "supposed to do" and assumed that any of my unhappiness was just the way it was meant to be. I lived trying to understand others' values and thought I could not significantly impact the culture of where I worked.

In 2001, however, my perspective shifted due to a tipping point incident. My boss at that time encouraged me to get out into the field and meet our national sales team face-to-face more often. He also gave me the OK to tap into a budget that had been set aside for me to travel. Following this advice, I attended a trade show in another city where many of our sales reps were making presentations. This not only gave me the chance to meet with them face-to-face but also to hear how they communicated the value of our products.

At one of the opening sessions and to my surprise, I saw my boss across the room as he had also chosen to attend the conference. He was there with the company president and came over for I what presumed would be a friendly chat. But the tone of the encounter quickly took a turn for the worse.

He curtly asked why I was there since they were trying to minimize the cost of the conference. When I reminded him of how he encouraged me to do such things, and that I was using my own budget, the logic did not sink in. He brusquely responded, "Well you can't step on your dick like that!"

I was shocked and left speechless by the comment. But looking back, I now know that my boss was under tremendous pressure from the company president; he felt he needed to show he was making a serious attempt at communicating the president's anger. He was actually one of my better bosses, and this type of behavior and language was not uncommon in company cultures in the 1980s and 1990s.

Tipping Point Leads to Personal Paradigm Shift
That moment in time with my boss also represented a personal tipping point...the beginning of my paradigm shift—from being the person I was supposed to be (a hard worker for the benefit of a company) to who I was meant to be—someone who could provide valuable advice to business leaders.

Never again would I allow myself to be in a situation that I felt I must be untrue to myself because of someone's power over me or their own view on reality. In a sense, that's when "Doug got back to being Doug!" Or maybe, "Doug started becoming Doug for the first time." I needed to muster up the courage to make a change.

I also started to realize at that time that I had suppressed many feelings for the first 44 years of my life—living my life the way I was "supposed" to and somewhat on other people's terms rather than on my own terms. In the supposed-to-do era, I worked for others, starting when I came out of college in 1979. I wanted to have a family with an above average lifestyle and some adventure. I thought computers were the future and found a job selling computers to banks. Banks have money, computers are the future, and I would not be stuck in an office; this seemed like what I was supposed to do so that I could build and support the family dream. Easy choice, right?

As this situation illustrates, many of us don't have the coaching and the tools nor the experience to figure out what we are meant to do. But as part of a large organization, I had learned about the culture and how I was supposed to behave to fit in and excel. I did this without thinking too much about what my beliefs were and whether they matched what I was supposed to do.

Often, when someone starts earning what they are capable of and growing a family, they start to feel locked-in to keep doing what they're supposed to do. If they need the money and don't feel there's an alternative, they tend to use their obligations as an excuse to not make a change.

But in the fall of 2001, I got the needed push and assistance to separate from my company. I wanted to figure out what the next phase of my life would look like and what type of career would meet my personal needs and desires. I documented every job I ever held, going way back to mowing lawns and selling Christmas cards as a kid. I noted what I liked and didn't like about each job—the bosses, the companies and the responsibilities (see Image #1 in the Appendix). This gave me the criteria for what I wanted for my future career.

With my last company, I had P&L responsibilities and traveled across the world. But at 44-years-old, I wanted next-to-no travel at all; I also wanted to be at home more often so I could go to my kids' events and not miss their youth. I came up with seven criteria for any opportunity I would consider for the future, and coaching business leaders hit on all seven.

This was the beginning of my career as a business coach!

Going to the Olympics

As I made the switch from the corporate world to working for myself as a business coach, I regularly came across forks in the road where I contemplated the "Supposed To Be" vs. "Meant To Be" choice. It's a challenging decision that can be difficult to make.

One such decision for me came in 2002 as I went through a personal self-discovery. A life-long friend of mine, who I ski raced with in high school, invited me to go to the Salt Lake Winter Olympics with former gold medal winner Bill Johnson, the first American gold medalist in the downhill (1984) who sadly passed away in early 2016.

At first I said I could not go—this was right when I was starting my new career in business coaching. I felt I shouldn't take the time nor spend the money. But I also realized I would never have the same chance again—to go to the Olympics and relive childhood dreams of becoming a world-class skier with my long-time friend.

So I "gave myself permission" to go!

This turned into a great time, I even saw my childhood hero Jean-Claude Killy, the famous French alpine skier, who was still living a vivacious life. On the airplane ride home after four wonderful days, I had this strange feeling. I had just finished an awesome vacation, but *I was not depressed*. I thought, why am I having these feelings?

It came to me immediately. Because I was going home......... "to Maine" to where I was meant to live, to start a new career that I was "meant to do."

The trip opened my emotions about the significance of making the transition to what I was meant to do—breathing-in the mountains and reconnecting with my youth and my passions cleared my head. It all came to fruition on the plane ride home as to just how much I had suppressed my feelings.

The Move from Ohio to Maine

After deciding to launch my business coaching business leaders, the next choice was where—Ohio or Maine. My wife Mary and I had grown up in Maine, and our parents still lived there. But we had lived in Ohio for 15 years, and our oldest son was going into his senior year in high school in the fall of 2002. Our second son was going into eighth grade, and our youngest son was about to enter third grade. We had a great house, great friends and a low cost-of-living. I had also established a network of business contacts.

Staying in Ohio would not disrupt the kids, and not moving meant no hassles. But not moving to Maine would prevent all of us from getting close again with our parents as well as cousins, aunts and uncles.

As we contemplated the decision, my wife asked: "10 years from now, if you look back, what will you feel more guilty about? Moving to Maine and messing up your son's senior year, or staying here and before we know it—our parents have passed away without our kids getting to know them or the rest of our family members?"

Looking at it from that perspective gave us the courage to move to Maine. This was a family decision of either doing what we were "supposed to" (stay in Ohio for the short term) or move to Maine for what we were "meant to do" for the long term. We worked towards the greater good, and the move turned out to bring us closer as a family. One son even wrote a paper for school about how the move to Maine helped him in his personal development.

How This Book Can Help You

I started off this book with these personal stories hoping to give you a real example of the "supposed to do" model versus the "meant to do" model and just how personal the transition from one to the other can be. As you now proceed with the rest of this book, it is primarily meant to help you evaluate where you're at in regards to the self-leadership of your business and your personal life, and to determine if you are living the way you were "meant to."

Perhaps you are unhappy and feel as though you can't change your situation. Or maybe things are pretty good, but you want to evaluate whether there's anything that can improve. It's also helpful to go through these exercises just in case something beyond your control changes without notice—such as the loss of a job or the loss of a loved one.

No matter your role in your current business or your family, the lessons within this book can help you grasp where you are now and where you want to go in the future—even it's just a little off the path you're currently on. It does not necessarily need to be as dramatic as the changes I went through where I changed careers and the place that I lived.

As a starting point, check out the Wheel of Life and Wheel of Business charts in the Appendix of this book (see Image #2 and Image #3). Within each slice, measure how satisfied you are. By self-assessing where you are today, you can determine how you're doing, how much control you have, and if you are happy with where you are in each slice of life.

It's important to proactively self-assess then consider concepts such as those put forth by the chapters of this book. The objective is two-fold; minimize your regrets and maximize your happiness!

As you read each chapter, you will find yourself better able to answer some of the toughest questions all of us should face periodically:

- Are you suppressing your feelings?
- Are you planning effectively for the future?
- Do you live a life of quiet desperation in some aspect of your life?
- Do you feel obligated to others—to the point where you sacrifice your own happiness?
- What keeps you fresh and pumped so you can give back and perform well for others?

Finding the answers to questions like these is important because you won't serve other people well if you are not being who you were meant to be. It's similar to what they always tell you right before an airplane takes off: Put your own oxygen mask on first before helping those next to you. You can't help others if you pass out. Your colleagues and your family will be much better off if you make sure you're the best that you can be by taking good care of yourself.

Each chapter stands as a lesson on its own, and you can use the book in any fashion that suits your needs. While you can read it all the way through in one sitting, it will likely help to tackle one chapter each month and work on that concept before moving onto the next. You may also want to pick out the chapters that resonate most strongly. You may find some chapters are more helpful than others.

Once you make your way through the entire book, I hope that you find it a handy reference that you want to keep at your fingertips. After all, self-improvement is a continuous process:

> Plan >> Do >> Learn >> Adjust
> (and then repeat!)

Even if you don't totally achieve all of your goals, you'll feel self-satisfaction knowing you stretched for greatness and were traveling in the right direction.

I wish you great happiness in your journey!

Doug

Chapter 1: Build Relationships—with Yourself and Others

As you assess your personal and your business relationships, both universes start with your relationship with yourself. You can only help others and interact with them effectively if you first work on the things you need and want to do for yourself. Just as we referred to in the Introduction, it's a lot like putting on your own oxygen mask first in the event of an airplane emergency. You can't help the person next to you if you pass out!

This chapter presents five key concepts in relation to building personal and business relationships:

1. Take care of yourself first...and realize you are not being selfish by doing so.
2. Prioritize your most important relationship.
3. Be intentional of who you invest time with.
4. Risk increasing the joy of your important relationships.
5. Develop habits, routines and rituals with each of your key relationships—including yourself.

As you consider my thoughts on each of these concepts, you may want to create one game plan for your personal life and another game plan for your business life. However, you may discover that one or two people will play key roles in in both.

Take Care of Yourself First
My dad's closest friend gave me a book when I turned 18, *As a Man Thinketh* by James Allen. The author was a Renaissance man—minister, author, poet, entrepreneur and counselor. But given my age

at the time, and that the book was written in old-style English, I did not give it much consideration.

Many years later after I married, my wife started collecting mini-books for a shelf in our bathroom. Coincidentally, the same book was part of this collection. I decided to give it a try and discovered two valuable concepts:

- You are what you think
- If you think you can, or if you think you can't—you're right!

That's when I realized my dad's friend had given me a great gift—the inspiration to believe in myself and the power of positive thought. Along a similar line, in the movie *The Bucket List*, the character portrayed by Morgan Freeman said life comes down to two questions:

- Have you found joy in your life?
- Has your life brought joy to others?

Considering these questions is the first step towards managing your relationship with yourself and plays a key role in managing your relationship with others. Taking care of yourself first allows you to be the best you can be for others. This holds true from a physical standpoint as well as a spiritual standpoint. You need to work on your own joy and your own fun to bring joy and fun to others.

As you ponder new ways to find joy and fun in your life, remember to consider both the personal and the business perspectives. You may find things are great in one role but not so much in the other. Where changes are needed, realize things won't improve overnight—just try to make yourself a little better each day than the day before by adopting an attitude built on three basic beliefs:

- Give yourself permission to take care of yourself
- Credit yourself for the things you do right
- Forgive yourself when you make a mistake

Don't harp too much on past mistakes, and don't over-worry yourself about what the future may hold. I believe in the concept that yesterday is history and tomorrow is a mystery, but today is the "present!" Work, Love and Play—and practice Gratitude every day. While it is important to learn from the past and plan for the future, don't over-think things, and don't get in your own way of enjoying each day.

Many people get caught in the trap of loving the life of serving others and putting themselves last. They have so many obligations that they can never say yes to having fun. They often wear "just how busy they are" as a badge of honor. It's almost as if they fear confronting themselves or giving themselves too much joy. In some cases they can become a martyr, spending all their time on the needs of others. In worst-case scenarios, they eventually blow up.

That's why it's so critical to find that delicate balance between doing things to replenish yourself and doing things for others.

Prioritize Your Most Important Relationship
After taking care of yourself, identify your single-most important relationship. Again, consider this from both the personal and the business perspective. Your number-one relationship in each area of your life likely plays a significantly-greater role than all your other relationships in the satisfaction and success you experience.

From the personal perspective, many people say their primary relationship (spouse, best friend, significant other) is the most important person in their life. But that's often not the way they live.

Their primary relationship becomes their business, their kids, a hobby or even an addiction.

It's important to step back and identify the number-one primary person in your life and make sure you proactively nurture that relationship. Be sure to fix anything that's broken and look for ways to keep nurturing the connection. Don't wait for something bad to happen and then find out it's too late to save the relationship.

Many people make their kids their primary focus. While it's true that kids should be your number-one responsibility and that there's great satisfaction in seeing them do well, they eventually go out on their own and focus on their own lives—as they should. Ideally, you want your primary relationship to be someone who also considers you to be their primary relationship and someone with whom you can be intimate—whether it's on an emotional, spiritual, social or physical level, or whether that intimacy covers the entire relationship spectrum.

I understand why some people view their kids as their primary relationship—I have three sons. But my wife is my most important relationship, even at the detriment of the kids. Your primary relationship is the person you will spend the most time with for the longest stretch of your life. Make sure that one is working well above all others!

Plan getaways and develop both common and diverse interests. Be sure to do some things together but also do some things independently. Strike a balance and keep communications open about all the things you do.

From the business perspective, you may want to sub-divide your world into categories, such as most important customer, most important employee (someone who reports to you, someone you report to, or someone who shares the same job), and your most important vendor. Be honest with yourself about who you value most and who means the most to your business life.

Also consider what you want from each person and what value you can provide to them. Then communicate the importance of your relationship and discuss what it will take to make sure it endures.

Unlike personal primary relationships—which we usually hope will last a lifetime—primary business relationships will likely have an ending when it no longer makes sense for both parties to continue working together. Proactively discussing an exit strategy and identifying the circumstances ahead of time as to when the business relationship may no longer be a win-win for both of you can make the eventual parting of the ways a lot less stressful. If things work out well, great business relationships that end can reinitiate on a future project and/or turn into personal relationships that endure.

For both your primary personal and business relationships, if anything is not working well, consider attending workshops or setting up counseling sessions. And even when things are working well, conduct a regular "Relationship Review & Celebration Meeting" to praise what is working well and discuss what can be improved. This helps both parties avoid focusing only on what isn't working, and instead take a larger perspective view of the value of the relationship and the aspects to be grateful for.

As you contemplate your primary relationships, truly search inside yourself. Be honest with what you are looking for and what you can offer. And realize that what you want and what you can offer can and will change over time.

Be Intentional of Who You Invest Your Time With

Now that you've considered your relationship with yourself as well as your most significant personal and business relationships, it's time to consider the other people you want to invest time with. You are the company that you keep, so prioritize who you spend that time with.

Start by ranking your top relationships—both personal and business. Be sure to take care of who matters most and get to know their needs, how their needs change, and what you are providing to them. By thinking of how you can improve the relationship, you can stay ahead of life and business changes.

Most people find it works best to create separate lists for business and personal relationships, but you may find a person or two that should be included on both lists. Perhaps a customer or vendor is also a good friend. Or maybe you and your spouse are business partners. As you consider relationships that span both your business and personal lists, create separate approaches for how you interact with that person.

When contemplating who is on your prioritized lists (which typically include 5-10 people or groups, such as multiple children and multiple close friends who might all rank together), consider who is a "bucket filler" and a "bucket emptier" when it comes to your emotions. Also consider whether they view you as a filler or an emptier.

Ideally, you want to spend your time with people for which both of you are fillers for each other. It can help to rank who you spend time with on scale of 1-10, with 1 signifying a major bucket emptier, and 10 representing your top bucket fillers. Then consider if the ranking for each person signifies a temporary phase or an on-going theme.

You don't want to spend too much time with people who tend to "cry on your shoulder" and vice versa. You will also discover some relationships you should back away from—those you can't improve at all. In some cases, you may decide to back away quietly without addressing the issue.

But then there will also be relationships you want to transform. Before approaching someone, consider these key questions:

- Do *you* need to change?
- Do *they* need to change?
- Do *both of you* need to change?
- How, when and where will you attempt to discuss the change(s)?

How you approach a major relationship transformation is key. Show them that you value the relationship and express gratitude for what you have done with and for each other in the past. Tell them your intentions going forward and be genuine.

It helps to be humble, and apologize if you contributed something negative to the relationship in the past. Also be sure to ask their feelings, set goals and consider multiple options. Seek first to understand, but also speak up if they are doing something that irks you. It likely irks others too, and if they are open to learning, they will appreciate your feedback.

One client I coached was very frustrated by a few of his problem customers. He felt like every time they said jump, he had to say, "How high?" I therefore led an educational session in his next peer-group session, called "Do Yourself a Favor, Fire a Customer."

The client went back to the office that day and wrote a list of eight customers that were not good customers. He called them himself and approached the subject tactfully. Two customers left, but he turned the other six into good customers. Not only did the company grow exponentially, which was great, but the best part was, he enjoyed his role as CEO more fully because he no longer felt like a victim.

Risk Increasing the Joy in Your Relationships

As you prioritize and work on the relationships you want to change, consider "taking a risk" at increasing the joy you get from each important relationship. These are situations where you realize something is not quite right or that there seems to be unresolved feelings between you and another person.

I know how much courage it takes to approach people. I used to be more introverted and would avoid conflict. But now I get disappointed in myself, and even upset at myself, if I avoid conflict.

When approaching people, how you deliver the message is a big factor. I set the table by letting them know my hopes, and I've found that people are usually open to discussing things. When you approach someone, you will likely discover that there's more to what you think has been going on than you realize. You may find out that you did not understand how that person truly feels.

By seeking to understand and leaving the righteousness at home, you will be amazed by what you discover. If you wait, it may be too late. If that person moves on, you will have lost the chance, perhaps forever. It also helps to have positive self-talks to psych yourself up when meeting with people and about to take on a challenging topic.

When I found out one of my closest friends was nearing the end of his life, I got on a plane the next day. We hugged each other and said we loved each other, and a week later he passed away. He was high on my priority list, and the week I spent with him prior to his passing away meant a lot to both of us.

When you take the risk of increasing the joy in one of your relationships, you also have to prepare for the possibility that the relationship might get worse. The person you approach may not be willing to tackle something that's coming between you.

But when you don't discuss things and take the risk to improve the relationship, you tend to look for evidence to corroborate your thoughts. You also look for negative confirmation and may misunderstand something.

And if you keep acting as though you are afraid or keep suppressing your feelings, something worse is likely going to happen anyway—you are just delaying the inevitable, or it will be an on-going unhealthy relationship for one or both of you. If your effort fails, at least you gave it a try and know inside that you went in with sincere intentions.

Develop Habits, Routines and Rituals

As you work to improve your key relationships, keep in mind that there's no such thing as overnight success. Improving any relationship takes time. The key is to proactively schedule regular interactions with the people you care about and to include them in some of your "take care of yourself" rituals. These can be something simple like walking the dog together, meeting for lunch, or exercising.

- What are your current habits, routines and rituals?
- Which ones work for you, which ones work against you?
- Do your habits, routines and rituals sync with those of your key relationships?
- Are there any bad habits you need to eliminate or reduce?

Another helpful ritual is keeping a gratitude list of what goes well each day. For my 30th birthday, my wife gave me a list of 30 things she loves about me, and I still carry it in my wallet. I also keep cards from my family, friends and clients and pull them out every now and then to remember how much they appreciate me.

It helps when you can be together with your key relationships, sharing quality time that's disconnected from distractions such as mobile phones and other electronic media. Get away from the places where you live and work, where it's easy to get distracted.

As philosopher Jim Rohn wrote..."Wherever you are, be there."

Taking this approach shows the people you are with that they are the most important person to you at that point in time. Just be with each other!

Maybe get away to a place of solitude, like playing golf, skiing or seeing a sunrise. Routines with friends, such as regular poker nights, may not get into deep conversations, but they build deep bonds where you know each of you will always be there for the others. It's not about poker—it's about being together.

A habit that I adopted with one of my sons was sharing a cup of coffee in the morning and watching a favorite comedy TV show before we both went off to work. This gave us a daily chance to share a laugh or two. I also developed a monthly ski date during the winter with my clients, prospects and friends. I invite people who are easy to be with, pick out one Wednesday each month, and the first three to sign up get to go!

Start Small and Don't Forget About Yourself
As with most major transformations in life, start small and gradually work your way up. You may identify many things you want and need to start doing for yourself, but trying to start them all at once will usually overwhelm you. Depending on what you decide to do, it may

make sense to try something new every three or six months, or perhaps as the seasons change.

When it comes to working on your relationships with others, focus on your primary personal and business relationships, and then turn to your other important relationships. But you can only do so much in the limited time you have. Don't spread yourself too thin that you start forgetting about yourself!

By the time you make your way to the fourth and fifth steps—taking risks for more joy in your relationships and developing habits, routines and rituals—you are at the stage when you can begin to alleviate the major sources of your stress regarding relationships that aren't quite right. And the regular interactions you schedule with the important people in your life will lead to even more joy as those interactions enable you to develop even deeper and more fulfilling relationships.

Chapter 2: Self-Management

Managing yourself often proves more challenging than managing others. Some people go too easy on themselves to appease their tendencies, and they simply give up on difficult challenges. They may also indulge in wasteful activities.

On the other end of the spectrum, some people tend to be much harder on themselves than they would ever dare to be with others. This can drive them to become burned-out or may lead to unhealthy addictions.

To help you take on this challenge, this chapter presents four key habits for effective self-management:

1. Develop and Maintain a Positive Attitude
2. Establish Personal Accountability
3. Seek Regular Feedback from Key Relationships
4. Conduct Objective Assessments to Identify and Measure Tendencies

The sections that follow present the key aspects to consider for each of the four habits along with some helpful tips to steer you in the right direction.

Develop and Maintain a Positive Attitude

It seems so simple, but developing a positive attitude involves a lot more than just turning on a switch. And maintaining a positive attitude requires consistent and proactive practice. But the effort is well worth it—about the only thing in life you can control is your own attitude, and nothing impacts self-management more than your attitude.

The effect can't be overstated. If your attitude is positive, you will generally experience good days. If your attitude is negative, you will generally experience bad days.

As the saying goes…"You are what you think!"

Some people view having a positive attitude as too much of a "Pollyanna" way of thinking—or seeing the world only with rose-colored glasses and missing the true reality. But a positive attitude does make people more successful and happier over time. Successful and happy people tend to be those who are better than others at maintaining a positive attitude.

When people are stuck, it's often because of their attitude—they give up or they think everything is against them. We all tend to compare ourselves to others, and if you do, you realize that there are some people that have more than you or are luckier than you.

But in most cases, there are many more people that have it worse. Watch the news and see how lucky we are just to live in the United States for example. By living here, we have it better than most of the world in many ways. If you find yourself feeling down, try doing some volunteer work. You will quickly discover just how much better off you are than many others—the effort puts things in perspective.

People who are good at self-management have a positive attitude almost all the time. They focus on and count their blessings often—not just when something tragic hits, but also as part of a regular routine, whether it's daily, weekly, or monthly. Doing so allows them to focus on what's good about their lives and helps them maintain a positive attitude.

Positive Attitude Tips: In addition to reading inspirational books, develop a ritual of pumping yourself up when going into important interactions with key relationships. Similar to how athletes prepare for a big game, it's no different in life and business. If you are about to walk into a big presentation to employees or about to interact on a tender subject with a family member, how you prep your attitude and how you look can be just as important as what you have to say: Perception is reality!

Also develop a weekly routine where you write down all your victories. Keep the list handy so that when something goes badly, you can pull out the list and quickly recover your attitude. Over time, you may be surprised at just how many great things you have achieved.

We all need motivation, and we need it often. Counting your blessings regularly makes it easier to lift yourself up when bad times hit; if you don't, it's much harder to pull yourself up.

To quote Zig Ziglar—the author, sales professional and motivational speaker: "People often say that motivation doesn't last. Well, neither does bathing- that's why I recommend it daily!"

Establish Personal Accountability

Personal accountability comes down to having the courage to "interrogate the reality" of both your personal life and business life as well as your own personal reality. When meeting with groups, I often like to start off by saying, "Today we're going to discuss both your favorite and your scariest subject, and they're the same...You!"

When you interrogate your own reality, seek first to understand yourself and any situation—don't show up all high-and-mighty. If you lose the ability to say, "How have I contributed to this situation, both positively and negatively," then you lose perspective and humbleness.

Keep asking, "What else could I have done and what could I have done better."

Personally, I have a little saying to myself; I know that I'll never rival Mother Theresa—but I also know I'm better than the devil! All I can do is learn and strive to be a better me than I was yesterday. I can only try to always do my best and celebrate my victories while also admitting my mistakes.

Seek to understand yourself as much as you seek to understand others. Evaluate how your tendencies help and how they hinder you from getting what you want in life. There's strength in being humble yet confident and open to learning; don't be overly confident or overly humble—strive for balance, even though it is easier said than done.

In the 1965 movie *Camelot*, Franco Nero, a very handsome, gifted Knight, who Guinevere falls in love with, sings a song about not expecting others to aspire to his level of greatness and humbleness. It's a funny but revealing example of a giving, loving person who is very self-confident and has many reasons to be rightfully so. But he lost his humbleness—even though he thinks he still has it!

Striking the humble yet confident balance applies to leaders, individuals and entire companies. Some reach a certain level of success and then get preachy (including me sometimes!). Strive to be comfortable in your own skin—not too hard on yourself, but also not too easy.

Personal Accountability Tips: Here are two tools you can use to sharpen your own Personal Accountability:

Decide to be the CEO of Your Life   17

- Envision a bullseye similar to an archery target as shown below that depicts your various States of Mind. The center shows challenges that fall in your comfort zone. These are the things you know you can accomplish fairly easily. The next ring out shows activities in your challenge zone—those that will take some stretching of your capabilities to accomplish. The third ring is your panic zone—the challenges you fear. For each business and personal challenge you face, determine where you are. What can you change to move closer to the center or at least leave your panic zone? Realize that if you don't have at least something in your life for which you are working in the challenge zone, your comfort zone will never get bigger. For your own personal growth, you need to be stretching in at least one aspect of your business and personal lives on an ongoing basis.

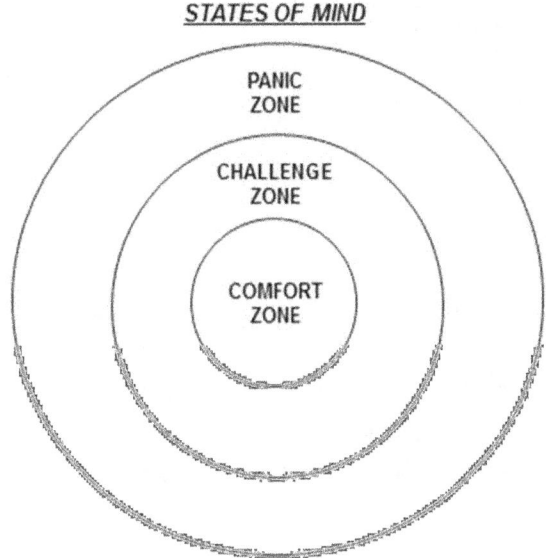

- Now envision the same bullseye—but this time the center is where you list things you can control while the next ring out is what you

can influence, and the third ring represents things you can't influence. Looking at your own Spheres of Influence, which aspects of a challenge fall into each zone? What can you do to control or influence a certain aspect? Who else could you partner with to influence or control an aspect? When working with others, you might be able to launch a plan you did not think of before.

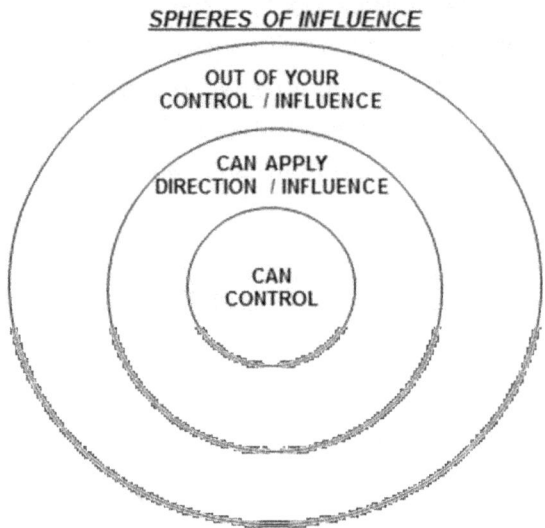

Most of the time, you don't have to try so hard to prove yourself to others, just be yourself. Those who spend too much energy trying too hard to prove themselves to others are seldom happy—in business or personally.

No one worth having in your life will want to be with you just because you drive a Ferrari!

Seek Regular Feedback from Key Relationships

We all need friends who can also be accountability partners. While some friends are superficial, many others genuinely care about us; we need true confidants that are willing to give honest feedback.

It takes time to initiate and develop these types of relationships, and you need to choose your accountability partners carefully. It's usually best to have reciprocal relationships where you provide feedback as well. Once you identify partners and have agreed to help each other, schedule regular feedback sessions. Feedback teams might meet less often depending on the relationships.

The feedback needs to come on a regular basis from your major business and personal relationships, and you need to know when it's coming. Consider setting up the feedback so that you get more in-depth at certain points throughout the year. Perhaps conduct monthly meetings that touch upon the prior month and annual meetings that review the entire year.

Providing and receiving feedback also requires balance: Like water, too much and you drown, too little and you die.

Feedback Tips: While it's best to work with feedback partners, you can also consider providing feedback to yourself if no partners are readily available at a particular point-in-time. Whether working on the process on your own or with others, here are a few guidelines to follow:

- For daily feedback sessions, consider what went well that day and how you can continue the pattern tomorrow.

- For weekly feedback, set aside time at the end or the beginning of your week; look back at what went well and what you need to adjust or improve.

- Monthly and quarterly sessions can go deeper, and you may want to incorporate feedback from other people or analyze any information you have that measures your effectiveness.

- Annual feedback sessions need to be a true time of reflection with yourself and others; to be effective, you need to get away from your regular environment. What are you doing in life and business, and what needs to change? One business leader I know goes away for two days every quarter and considers the ideas his employees submitted. He reads, reflects and comes back ready to shift gears strategically and tactically.

- To ensure the feedback sessions take place, establish a calendar at the beginning of the year and stick to it, even if you are not fully prepared for a particular session. You and your feedback partner(s) will likely learn from your sessions and make them better over time.

As you go through the feedback process, try to receive diverse input from people who present differing views; and make sure you welcome feedback without putting up barriers that might prevent people from being completely open.

Simply put, shut-up and listen! Ask only clarifying questions and don't be defensive. The best leaders are also great followers. Sometimes, you need to let others lead while you serve as a good listener, contributor and follower.

Also consider each piece of feedback you receive within the context of other feedback. People often don't have filters and just blurt out "Do this or don't do that." Consider their feedback carefully, but also weigh their advice against your values and your gut.

Conduct Objective Assessments to Identify and Measure Tendencies

Where feedback tends to be subjective and biased, another aspect to consider in the self-management process is the use of formal assessments, which tend to be objective. Periodic assessments can help you identify your tendencies and measure your satisfaction with particular aspects of your life.

These can be assessments you take on your own, such as the Wheel of Life and Wheel of Business charts referred to in the Introduction. What areas are you happy with and which ones are you willing to take a stab at improving? Doing such assessments on an annual basis is a major step forward in making actual changes.

Over time, utilize multiple assessments to look at yourself and your business in different ways. Even a single question can be an assessment unto itself if you break it down into objective answers.

You can simply try starting with, "Am I Happy?"

To expand your assessments, there are many types of intelligence measurements to consider. In 1983, developmental psychologist Howard Gardener described nine types:

- Naturalist (nature smart)
- Musical (sound smart)
- Logical-mathematical (number/reasoning smart)
- Existential (life smart)
- Interpersonal (people smart)

- Bodily-kinesthetic (body smart)
- Linguistic (word smart)
- Intra-personal (self-smart)
- Spatial (picture smart)

Depending on what you want to work on most in your life, you might consider assessments in one, a few or all nine of these areas.

While you do need a reasonable amount of intelligence, intelligence is not really the primary factor that takes you higher in succeeding from a happiness standpoint. Your level of emotional intelligence plays a bigger role. This measures your ability to interact with yourself, others and groups. Emotional intelligence assessments can help improve facilitation and collaboration skills, which increases your effectiveness and your happiness. You can't really increase your natural intelligence, but you can increase your emotional intelligence. There are books and assessments available on emotional intelligence—I use and recommend them often.

Assessment Tips: As you conduct assessments to help take on the challenges you face, consider that there's usually more than just you involved. You may need to bring people together to define the situation, the real causes, the options for solving the situation, and then get together as a team to solve it. This dynamic can occur with just yourself, with one other person, or with a group. The key is to keep discovering and keep learning.

People tend to use assessments to identify their weaknesses and then work on them. Many people spend a lot of time doing things they don't like and are not very good at. As one of my CEO clients said, "Find out what you're not good at, and don't do it!"

But it may be more important and more effective to identify your strengths, which can also be more difficult to determine. Consider resources such as *StrengthsFinder* 2.0 by Tom Rath, which also gives you access to an online test. When you discover your strengths, you can then build them into real value-differentiators and maybe even create your legacy. The more you get to know yourself through assessments, the easier it is to make choices that will increase your effectiveness and happiness.

There's an endless array of tests online for just about anything. Many people like the Myers-Briggs behavioral assessment, which has been around a long time, but there are hundreds you can consider—some that cost money but many that are free or come with the purchase of a book.

The important thing is to use a variety and to pick those that focus on areas you want to improve. For example, I take the same assessments as my clients so we can talk the same language.

Although some people tend to over-analyze themselves, assessments can be very helpful on a periodic basis, perhaps once or twice per year. As you build your strengths and mitigate your weakness, also surround yourself with people who have complementary skills and celebrate the diversity among your key relationships.

Your Future Is More Important Than Your Past

At the end of the movie *Chapter 2*, based on the play by Neal Simon, James Caan reads the opening line of his new book to his new wife: "Bill Smith awakes, drags himself to the mirror, and sees what he fears most: Bill Smith."

While it's important to face yourself, don't beat yourself up too much! What you have done in the past is not nearly as important as your vision and what you will accomplish in the future. In this scene from the movie, Bill was beating himself up about the death of his first wife, but he then learned to get over it.

With effective self-management, you too can learn to overcome what's not optimal in your life and take on your biggest challenges—with the positive outlook that you *will* succeed.

Chapter 3: Set Goals to Plan for Success

We often hear about the importance of setting and achieving goals, but many people struggle with the process. Some simply can't bring themselves to the point where they can actually create goals while others over-analyze how to achieve their goals to the extent that they never start their action plans.

Perhaps the first step is to understand why it's important to set goals...

Life is short, and without goals it's easy to let people and the things that are important slip away. You don't want to arrive at the end only to discover you wasted opportunities and skills, and that you did not achieve or experience the things you really wanted.

A great saying I once came across perhaps puts it best: "Life Is Ephemeral; Don't Waste It Looking Up Long Words!"

To help those unfamiliar with the word (and to keep you from wasting time!), ephemeral means *fleeting*. Many people spend so much time without a plan or clear goals that they end up spending the majority of their time on mind-numbing, fleeting and wasteful activities.

Setting and achieving goals is important because doing so also leads to happiness. A common attribute of happy people is that they are better planners than most. They succeed by following an on-going process to help them reach their goals.

Here's one I recommend that might work well for you:

1. Set Clear Goals

2. Plan>>Do>>Learn>>Adjust (in relation to both the goal and the steps towards achieving the goal)
3. Develop Habits, Routines and Rituals (to keep momentum in advancing towards your goals)
4. Ask for Help Along the Way (you may be surprised how many people want to help)
5. Schedule Rejuvenation (take time-outs to have fun and celebrate victories)

As you set off on your own goal-setting and planning journey, remember that the difference between ordinary and extraordinary is just a little "extra" effort. If your goals are just little bit more clear, a little more of a stretch, and a little more intentional, it's not only more inspirational for you but also for others—particularly if your goals impact those around you.

Set Clear Goals

To paraphrase comments by the Cheshire Cat in *Alice in Wonderland* by Lewis Carroll, "If you don't have a clear destination, it doesn't matter which road you take next."

Even if you create a short-term goal as simple as helping out at a local shelter once per month, stating it clearly and succeeding improves your self-esteem and self-image. Success also attracts other people to you—they see you are self-driven and want to help.

As you work on creating your goals, break them down into your personal life and your professional life. Perhaps begin with what you want to accomplish by the time you retire. Then break the goals down into annual, quarterly, monthly and perhaps weekly and daily checkpoints along with activities to make appropriate progress towards each goal during the given time period.

If you want to lose 25 pounds, you might give yourself one year to achieve the goal, but you will want to schedule at least weekly checkpoints. If you want to obtain a net worth of $1M, you may very well need to give yourself 10 or 20 years or even more time. But along the way, you'll need to check on your progress on a regular basis.

For some, reaching the stage where they can start to think about setting goals takes a major life disaster or life change, such as the passing of a parent. Fear of failure also keeps people from setting goals. But if you set your goals in a way that's a bit of a stretch, falling short does not necessarily mean you have failed.

If you strive to save $1 million, for example, but "only" reach $500,000—is that such a bad thing?

A client of mine set a career goal of writing for the Wall Street Journal. He has not made it quite that far…just yet. But he has advanced his career several rungs upward and is a very successful journalist at a major newspaper. By creating a stretch goal, he moved beyond his comfort zone and achieved much more than if he had settled on a less ambitious, comfortable goal.

When you reach the point where you set clear goals, you will be surprised how the necessary tactics and strategy soon become clearly apparent as well. That's because a clear goal allows you to think more deeply. It's easier to think about what you need to get there, and you begin talking about your goals to others.

Before you know it, they will start to offer you help as well!

> This set of SMART goal attributes can help you measure the clarity of your goals:
>
> - **S**pecific
> - **M**easurable
> - **A**ctionable
> - **R**ealistic
> - **T**ime-bound

Tips for Setting and Achieving Goals

As you go through the process of setting and achieving personal and professional goals, here's a set of tips to get you started and keep your momentum moving forward:

Tip 1: Create Goal Folders—Assemble your notes and resource materials for each goal on your computer or in a hard-copy folder. Brainstorm the steps you need to take and then sequence the steps. Also create blocks of time on your calendar to work on each goal. The folder helps you track what you have already done and reminds you of what you need to do next to achieve the goal. Also make notes on who can help with each step or the entire goal and other resources you might need.

Tip 2: Track and Segment Goals—As goal ideas pop into your head, write them down in a four-quadrant chart like the one below, placing each goal in the appropriate quadrant. This will make sure you don't forget to pursue any goals that are important and also helps you prioritize and segment what to work on.

	Professional	**Personal**
Short-Term	• Attend sales training course to increase percent of closed prospects to 75%. • Lean how to maintain the company's general ledger to ensure required cash flow. • Hire an assistant to offload administrative tasks and focus more time on core activities.	• Schedule regular time with adult children—at least once per month. • Develop consistent work-out routine—every-other-day. • Improve golf game to start shooting 80 or better.
Long-Term	• Move home office into a productive business office setting. • Expand business to include 10 employees. • Generate annual revenues of $1M per year.	• Create and maintain long-term savings/investment plan for retirement: Attain net worth of $1M. • Establish vision of what a life of retirement will look like. • Visit Hawaii and the California wine country.

Tip 3: Plan>>Do>>Learn>>Adjust—For this process, determine the easiest route to accomplish each goal and then sequence the steps you will need to take. Schedule a 15 minute-appointment with yourself at the beginning of each day and plan the three professional and personal tasks you want to get done that day—those that are the most important activities in achieving your goals. As other things get in the way, as they always do, you can then stay focused on the top three that are most important.

While it may seem difficult to set aside time each day, consider the challenge facing Kerri Walsh Jennings, the Olympic volleyball player who won medals in four straight Olympics from 2004 to 2016. Along the way, she gave birth to three children and found it challenging to balance family needs with training needs. To help reach her goals, she decided to wake up each day 90 minutes before the family, meditate, and then plan her day. This helps her keep things on schedule and achieve both her family and her professional goals.

Tip 4: Develop Habits and Routines—By understanding your personal rhythms, you can match your routines and habits to your rhythms. A CEO that I coach works many hours each day including evening events. She was not exercising and thus felt stressed. As we talked about her personal rhythms, she realized she was not a productive morning person, so she started going to yoga classes three days each week in the morning and then went to work just a little later in the day. She is now more productive at work and has more energy. She also still attends evening business events but feels refreshed. She essentially gave herself permission to take care of herself.

In developing habits and routines to plan and achieve your goals, you will need to determine the best times of the day, the best days of the week and the best times of the year to think reflectively. Whether it's the morning or late at night, during the weekends, or at the beginning of each calendar year, we all tend to have moments during which we can focus our thoughts more clearly. Going back to my memories as a child, September and the new school year came to represent the beginning of a new year for me. With the summer just about over and the crisp fall air about to set in, this time of year has always worked well for me as a time for annual planning.

Tip 5: Keep Goals Visible and Celebrate Victories—This can be done using the quadrant referenced above or a simple goal sheet you post near your desk. Keep referring to the list and updating your progress towards each goal rather than starting a new update list each time. Also set rewards for achieving your goals or your actions leading up to a goal. For example, you might go big by buying a new car to celebrate achieving an annual revenue goal. But you can also go small—such as getting a task done before noon and giving yourself the simple reward of taking the dog for a walk.

Tip 6: Stretch Your Comfort Zone—To create goals that stretch your comfort zone, envision an archery target where the inner circle represents what's in your control (the comfort zone). The second ring represents what you can influence (the stretch zone) and the third what you can't influence (beyond your capabilities). This is similar to the image we discussed in the Self-Management chapter. You can usually achieve a lot more than you think, and if you don't push yourself into the stretch zone, your comfort zone will never get bigger. If you plan how you will approach something and go about it with authenticity, you'll be amazed at how much people will help and how much your courage will increase.

Plan Your Work and Work Your Plan

In the movie, *The Fundamentals of Caring*, Paul Rudd is a caregiver for a young man with muscular dystrophy who would not leave his house. But Rudd urged him to go beyond his comfort zone, and the young man learned that he could achieve so much more than he ever dreamed.

They went on a road trip where the young man got to see many new sights and even met the woman of his dreams as Rudd helped push him into his stretch zone. Some of us might consider a date with the person of our dreams to be reaching our panic zone!

This is a great example of how sharing your goals with others can lead to them providing you with the push you need. As you stretch your goals, avoid the main roadblocks, which are lack of clarity and not moving forward on the Plan>>Do>>Learn>>Adjust process. To succeed, you also need to make sure you develop good habits and routines, ask for help, and rejuvenate often!

Remember, success in life is usually a series of sprints, not a marathon. Work diligently at your goals in small blocks of time and then take breaks rather than trying to plow through long stretches and going the distance all at once. By consistently planning your work and working your plan, you're much more likely to realize your dreams.

Chapter 4: Manage Your Energy and Your Focus

A key challenge just about everybody runs into on a daily basis is trying to manage their energy and their focus in order to reach their full productivity potential. At one point or another in each day, we tend to get distracted by the priorities and urgencies of others as well as our own wandering thoughts.

An approach that can help solve this challenge is to establish consistent habits, routines and rituals. These allow you to not only maintain your own rhythm as you progress through each day but also help those you work with understand the best ways to interact with you so that you and they can work more productively together.
As you develop your habits, routines and rituals, gear them towards managing three primary objectives:

1. Limit Your Accessibility to Others
2. Manage Your Use of Electronic Devices
3. Avoid Guilty Feelings for Not Keeping "Busy" All the Time

Success in the first two objectives enables you to limit the distractions that keep you from reaching your full productivity potential. Success in the third objective is necessary for helping you relax, have fun, and to focus more of your time on strategic planning.

Limit Your Accessibility to Others
This area relates to the access you give to the people you work with as to how often and when they can knock on your office door or call your phone. It's a difficult balance trying to find what works well for you and your staff.

Going back more than 20 years or so, leadership tended to take a closed-door, intimidation approach: Don't bother the boss unless you have good news!

But the business world has since transformed into an environment where the managers believe they must be accessible and their door always open. People tend to share everything—from their business lives to their personal lives. Thus, today's boss is expected to always be accessible and open to constant interruptions. Each person in the company is important in their moment of need.

Given their extremes, both approaches have their drawbacks. The key is to strike a balance somewhere in the middle. That means scheduling regular heads-down time where you're not accessible unless there's a true emergency. This enables you to get your own work done and spend time in a creative thinking/planning mode. You can then have a more open mind and go up to the 10,000-foot view to analyze what's working, what's not, and to create a vision for your company. You can truly focus on what's most important, not just what is urgent.

A great tool in managing your accessibility is to coach your team to think before approaching you. Also ask them to think about possible solutions. Having them complete the quick exercise that follows can greatly facilitate the process:

- Define the issue or opportunity.
- Why is it important?
- If it's an opportunity, what impact will success have on the company?
- What happens if we fail?
- If it's an issue, what is the root cause?
- What are the options for solving the issue or taking advantage of the opportunity?
- Which option do you recommend and why?

- What's the best next step?

When people work their way through these steps, it helps ensure they come through your door ready to talk and proceed efficiently. In some cases, they may realize that email is the better way to communicate, and the process may even allow them to solve the issue on their own—without consulting with you at all!

But even if they don't solve their issue, they're at least giving you a head start on working through the process. You and they can then both proceed much more efficiently.

Manage Your Use of Electronic Devices

When your mobile phone battery runs low on power, do you feel tired too?

As bizarre as these sounds, many of us are virtually joined at the hip to our electronic devices. I like to refer to this objective as the 'Digital Detox' process—where you schedule time to disconnect completely from all your phones, all your computers and any other electronic devices. Many of us don't realize how addicted we've become to "smart" devices that bring us to the Internet in an instant for communications and information. It's important to take time every now and then to just be with yourself and other people.

During my annual canoe trip with clients who are also my friends, we explore the Saco River in Maine where there's no mobile phone reception at all. At the beginning of the trip, we all turn off our phones and put them away. It feels so refreshing to spend time with friends and nature. It also allows our minds to go into neutral and feel very relaxed.

Another game I like to play when going out to dinner with business associates is to have us all put our phones on the table face down. The first one to touch their phone has to pay for dinner!

While it's not always easy to proactively plan for disconnect time away from your mobile phone, email and other electronic distractions, it's absolutely critical to do so. It's the only way to truly refresh your brain and allow yourself to think clearly.

When you're disconnected, you can still establish an emergency communications protocol for the people who are most important to you. But by letting them know of your disconnect times and/or communication habits ahead of time—such as checking email once in the morning and once in the afternoon—they can learn when it's best to contact you.

As you educate others on how to communicate with you, also commit to always getting back in touch within a certain amount of time, such as no more than half a business day or the next business day.
You don't have to always drop things and get back to them in five minutes. That approach takes away energy and focus and allows others to determine your priorities.

Some business leaders fear that taking this approach may appear to be too pompous, but you're actually helping people get the best from you. If on the other hand you always answer right away, you may look good in the moment, but you may also look like you don't have other priorities or a personal life. Your staff and customers will expect you to answer them right away—all the time.

An investor that one of my clients partners with gave the company a presentation on how to communicate with him so that he could proactively manage their expectations. He made his idiosyncrasies known, such as "don't deliver bad news on a Friday—I work hard during the week but want to enjoy my weekends!"

He also advised them not to contact him before 9am—that part of the morning was reserved for his workouts and mental prep for the day. By informing them of his routines, the investor maximized his own productivity and his value to the company. He also provided a great example as to how others could manage their own communications in a similar fashion.

Avoid Guilty Feelings

The natural tendency is for people to want to be busy and needed; if they don't stay busy, they think they're failing. But then they complain that they don't have time for strategic planning. Even more importantly, they don't have time for fun.

When people tell me they haven't played much golf or haven't done anything fun lately, I say, "That's just poor planning!"

Some people think being "busy" is good. If they spend quiet time planning or enjoying activities such as golf, they feel guilty—as though they can't prove to themselves and others that they are getting things done.

The ultimate objective in spending quiet time to plan strategy for your company and to rejuvenate is to work yourself out of your job—by giving others the tools they need to succeed in your roles. A good way to manage your guilt is to consider the paradigm of Value vs. Time. The amount of Time you spend does not equate to the Value of what you do.

Consider the case of the large manufacturing company with a mission-critical machine on the assembly line that has broken down. No one in the company can get it to work. They call a specialist who spends two minutes assessing the machine and then tapping a small spot with a tiny hammer. The machine immediately starts to work.

When the specialist sends a bill for $10K, the manufacturing company complains. "How can you bill us that amount for two minutes of your time?"

The specialist calmly responds: "I'm charging you $1 for my time and $9,999 for knowing where to tap."

Creating value like this—that's seemingly delivered in a small amount of effort—does not happen overnight. It takes time to develop the expertise to deliver value efficiently. It also takes time to develop relationships that lead to valuable business connections. Strive to provide the appropriate amount of value in the minimum amount of time required, and remember, knowledge is more valuable than the actual time spent on resolving an issue.

When increasing your personal value, it takes guts and a stick-to-it attitude to avoid guilty feelings. But the reward is worth so much more than the risk. As effective leaders take the time to plan and rejuvenate, they don't need to kowtow to anyone who complains: you took the risk to get where you are, and when enjoying recreational activities with customers and vendors to build relationships, there's no need to feel guilty. In fact, feeling guilty is detrimental to you and your business.

Your time away from the business could be for other personal reasons as well. Another business leader I work with home-schools her kids, so she's at the office only 24 hours per week. Leaders all need and deserve time away from work—no matter the reason.

A neat exercise is to envision spending time away from the business: What would you do? A business owner that I coach spends every Friday at home. The mornings are for planning and strategizing while the afternoons are earmarked for doing something fun—whether it's with customers and business partners or family and friends.

Take the proactive mindset to enjoy your time away from work and always remember that keeping busy is not always better. You can find that balance to achieve your financial goals but still enjoy time away with family and friends. These times can be even more ideal if your customers and business partners are also your friends!

Helpful Tips for Mitigating Distractions

Here are a few suggestions to decrease the number and duration of distractions and energy-draining challenges that you face. Taking these steps can help you focus your energy where it's needed most.

- **Create uninterrupted, closed-door times**—These might be two, one-hour segments per day. Make your staff aware of these times. One executive I work with only schedules the first half hour of any given hour for meetings so he can take the second half of the hour to work on the results.
- **Put electronic communications out of sight**—Make it impossible to hear and see all the incoming emails, text messages and phone calls. This is also important when you meet with people. It shows you are giving them your undivided attention.
- **Set up the layout of your office to minimize distractions**—Place your desk so you face away from the door and windows where you can see people walking by. Also be sure to de-clutter your office, create a simple filing system and limit the mementos on your desk. Anything within your sight is sure to distract.
- **Create a four-quadrant to-do list**—Rather than one long list, use a four quadrant format with "Business" and "Personal" on one side

and "Short-Term" and "Long-Term" on the other. This helps get everything on your mind onto paper and helps you prioritize what you need to do in a given time period.
- **Work in cycles**—Think of each day as several sprints rather than one marathon. Take short breaks between tasks by walking, stretching, reading an article or taking care of a personal action item. Reward yourself for the heads-down work and don't deplete yourself. Save part of the day for non-work activities.
- **Do the most difficult thing first**—If you don't, it will be on your mind all day. It usually doesn't turn out nearly as bad as you think!
- **Work on one thing at a time rather than attempting to multi-task**—Strive to complete two or three things each day that are most critical so you have a sense of accomplishment. This is much more energizing than partially completing many tasks, which usually proves to be frustrating.
- **Help others minimize the drag they place on your time**—This includes giving people time limits for meetings. Consider using formats or forms for people to submit before meeting on the topic they want to discuss, why it's important, the options and their recommendations. This will likely require you to coach your staff, but in the long run, it saves a ton of time.

Enjoy the Journey Along the Way

One of my client's mottos is, "Be brief, be bold, be gone." Make your decisions on how to develop habits, routines and rituals and then act. Don't procrastinate your decision-making—perhaps you can even accelerate your decisions!

Chances are good you'll learn as you go and improve your approach. Over time, you're sure to reach success in managing your accessibility, your use of electronic devices, and your guilt. You may also come to know what a client of mine once said quoting his dad: "It's lonely at the top, but you eat better."

Be sure to enjoy your journey along the way!

Chapter 5: Maximize Your Return-On-Time

Business leaders regularly measure the return of their monetary investments, but it's just as important to measure and maximize your R.O.T or Return-On-Time. It's a term that came to me from one of my clients, who said to me, "You not only have helped me improve my ROI....You have helped me increase my R.O.T....my Return-On-Time...on this earth."

The way in which he emphasized the second part of his statement is one of the most satisfying moments of my coaching career. Our time here on earth is truly precious. Proactively managing your time not only improves your performance and your quality of life, but also sets an example for those you work and live with. They too can benefit from your time-leadership attributes.

Why is it important to maximize your R.O.T? Because if you don't prioritize your time, someone else will!
Time is the only thing we all have the same amount of. Much of leadership effectiveness, and your happiness, is based on how you invest your time.

But many people get caught in their own "time management chaos" where they feel compelled to do certain things and can't change. While daily time management is important, time leadership involves creating what could be or should be—in order to increase life satisfaction and to fulfill your desire to be more fulfilled. This means working smarter, not harder.

Here's a high-level planning model that works well for me...

- During the week, I plan my fun around my work.
- During the weekends, I plan my work around my fun!

Each weekend, I schedule a couple fun things for rejuvenation, and then schedule the work I can get done around those things so I won't ruin the fun.

One of my proactive choices is working smarter so I can play more golf. By the end of the golf season, I typically have played about 40 rounds whereas others I talk to who also love golf have only played a couple times or perhaps not at all. I firmly believe...it's truly all about how well you plan and what you give yourself permission to do.

I plan my golfing schedule to combine it with business-generation and networking activities—such as a Tuesday night league with business owners. On the weekends, I play early in the morning to exercise with friends and to do more business networking. I'm then back home by noontime to enjoy the rest of the weekend with my wife and to take care of things around the house.

This approach works much more effectively than waiting until Saturday morning to make a plan for the weekend. Chances are good you will get bogged down by the list of things you have to do, and before you know it, there's no time or you're too tired for rejuvenating activities.

Making the Case for Change

Time is precious. Proactive planning is absolutely necessary to maximize your performance and your joy. Consider the allegory of the professor who places a big, empty pickle jar on his desk. He first puts several large stones in the jar and asks the class if the jar is full. They all say, "Yes."

He then pours in pebbles around the large stones and asks if the jar is now really full. Again, they say, "Yes" but with a little hesitation.

The professor then pours in sand to completely cover the stones and the pebbles. Now the jar is really full—right? No! He then pours in water that fills the jar.

This story illustrates how people tend to focus on the small pebbles and even the sand—representing the minutiae of life that bombards all of us. It's easy to lose track of the big rocks. You can't even see them in the jar anymore, let alone realize they're still there!

That's why it's important to pause and determine what's important. Make sure you identify and work on the "big rocks" in your life before the pebbles and the sand get in the way of maximizing the time you spend on what's truly important.

Set Priorities—Remove Excuses

The pace of change and information-overload can cause us to run harder rather than stopping to assess how to run smarter. We have so much to do that we keep our heads down without coming up for air.

People often get themselves into this situation by giving too much accessibility to other people—both in our business life and our personal life. We leave our "doors" open too much of the time.

People also tend to plug into digital devices nearly the entire time they're awake, and some leave them on even when they're asleep! Whether it's the mobile phone, desktop, laptop, notebook or television, these devices distract our focus and drain our energy.

In some cases, people are drawn to "wearing the badge of being busy." They take pride in appearing to have so much to do that they can't take time to "get centered" or have any fun.

The end result: Jars fill up with pebbles, sand and water—and there's no time left for the big rocks!

The first step in establishing effective time leadership is setting priorities. This step links back to goal setting and reflecting on the Wheel of Life and the Wheel of Business charts we presented in the opening chapter (see Image #2 and Image #3 in the Appendix). After filling out the two charts, you can then step back to reflect and plan:

- Where are you not seeing the results you want?
- How will you adjust your investment of time in each area?
- What have you learned about yourself and your career?
- How do your past learnings change your goals, your plans and your metrics of success?
- How will you adjust your business and personal schedule to achieve those plans?

When I transitioned to a career as a business leader coach, I determined the characteristics that my next opportunity needed to provide in order to fulfill my goals. Among my seven criteria within my

Opportunity Matrix (see sample in the Appendix), schedule flexibility/control was my number-one priority.

As you decide which changes your life requires, you can go further into your own Opportunity Matrix and use other tools to determine criteria, such as whether or not to change where you live. When you succeed, you will discover that controlling your schedule is very valuable and rewarding.

Tactics for Improving Time Leadership

Reflect>>Plan>>Do—Effective leadership requires regularly-scheduled time to Reflect>>Plan>>Do. Some people reflect too long and procrastinate their planning and doing. Others don't reflect enough, and they skip right over planning and into the doing—which more often than not creates poor results.

To help you strike the right balance, here are a few tips:

- The time spent on each of the Reflect>>Plan>>Do steps needs to be uninterrupted.
- Decide how often to perform each step, where, and what tools you will use.
- Determine your goals and then develop strategies, tactics and actions to achieve those goals.
- Schedule enough time to do what you need to do in order to achieve the goals; this may require regularly-scheduled sessions each week or each month, and perhaps bigger chunks of time every six months or every year.

Also break out the time you assign to goals into different types—work, family, fun—instead of trying to blend them together during the same time periods.

Accountability Partner—A great way to work through the Reflect>>Plan>>Do process is to collaborate with an accountability partner or a team. Tell them your intended changes and invite them to do the same for themselves. Then share and support each other with your progress and clearing your hurdles. The partner(s) could be a friend, a coach, a pastor, or a team of confidants. Asking them to help you achieve your goals is much like a workout buddy, someone who keeps you going and can even serve as a friendly competitor.

Multi-Year Calendar—Another tactic is to utilize a multi-year calendar for major goals so that if someone tells you they can't do something, you still make it happen in the future. One of my clients, who has several nieces and nephews, proactively tries to schedule get-togethers with each of them on her calendar over the next 12 months. If one of them says they can't, she asks about the following 12 months. When asking a niece if she could go to Italy later that year, the niece said she couldn't. So my client then asked if she could go the following year, and the niece said yes. This gave both of them time to think and dream about the trip and save up money. Ever since that interaction, my client has kept a multi-year calendar and doesn't let scheduling be an excuse for not accomplishing items on her "bucket list."

Weekly Meetings—Weekly meetings with your family and your business teams are also good tools for helping you prioritize so you can manage your time appropriately. My family did this for years when the kids were young and then again when two of them moved back home as adults. The idea came from an annual personal planning day that I lead with my clients. One of my clients said, "You know how when you occasionally get out to dinner with your spouse, and you end up talking about the kids, and the "business of running the family"? Well, we finally got back to making those dinners real dates. We did this by holding Sunday Night Family Business meetings. We get together early Sunday night—when everyone tends to be at home—and talk about what everyone has going for the upcoming week. This includes finding out who needs what help and who will agree to help. This also lets us schedule that week's date night for me and my wife, family chores, and even some family fun time. The weekly meetings help eliminate surprises and frustration over schedules and responsibilities.

Bucket Fillers and Bucket Emptiers—In addition to regular weekly and monthly meetings, I also recommend an annual Bucket Filler/Bucket Emptier Review—as discussed in an earlier chapter. Once each year, make a list of the people you spend time with who fill your bucket and who empty your bucket. You might even do this exercise as a couple. Decide which relationships are worth expanding or saving, and thus worth investing more time in. Also consider which ones are worth cutting lose or spending less time with.

As you go through the process, also consider for whom you are a bucket filler and a bucket emptier. Perhaps there's someone with whom you want to make a change—one way or the other. Many people avoid these conversations, but as the book *Fierce Conversations* by Susan Scott presents, having those tough conversations gets to the heart of the matter in a way that deepens relationships worth saving or expanding.

Strategic Calendaring—A tactic that helps with long-term planning is to create a Strategic Calendar for Responsibilities and Time Allocation (as shown in the Appendix—Image #4) that shows work and personal responsibilities:

- Where do you spend your time now?
- Where do you want to be a year from now?
- Where do you want to be eventually?

As you plan a month, determine the percentage of time you want to spend on each responsibility. You can then determine how to break down your time for each day of an upcoming month. From there you can schedule the time you need with other people as well as the time you need with yourself.

Using the monthly calendar view from the Strategic Calendar for Responsibilities and Time Allocation, enter the percentage of time you decide to invest in each responsibility. Then calculate the total time per month you will spend on each responsibility. You can break down the total time for business roles across the 20 business days in the month, and personal time can be scheduled across all 30 days. You can then schedule activities on your calendar and book time with the required people.

As you adjust and unplanned things come up, you will immediately know the number of hours you need to reallocate as the month progresses. At the end of the month, you can see how well you did in prioritizing your responsibilities and adjust the next month accordingly.

I try to schedule 90-minute coaching sessions with each client once per quarter, and I calendar out my coaching days for the year to make travel efficient. I then offer the calendar to all of my clients with slots going to whoever responds first.

I also include the hint that 1 p.m. slots in warm weather are great for golf! That's a win/win for both of us—there's nothing better than spending time on something fun with a current client or a prospect.

Utilizing a strategic calendar such as the one this model presents provides several key benefits:

- Matches your time investment with your priorities.
- Provides context for decisions about adding to your calendar before taking on new responsibilities—so you will realize when you need to drop something else or say no to lower priorities.
- Improves your willingness to eliminate responsibilities, realizing you don't have enough time for everything and identifying responsibilities you may be able to delegate.
- Helps you set time management examples for others to emulate; others need to invest their time properly too, and you don't want to hand over a mis-managed business role to someone else.

Strategic calendaring also helps you make sure you're where you're supposed to be and at the right time. It increases your ability to live by Rohn's quote: "Wherever You Are, Be There."

Striking a Balance Across the Lead-Manage-Do Model

Leaders need to spend most of their time planning, investigating opportunities, determining improvements, managing relationships, and giving back to the community. But they also need to allocate part of their time for managing and coaching direct reports. In some cases, leaders will also want to add more of their time back into the front lines so as to not lose touch with customers and employees. You want to work toward investing most of your time leading but can't forget the other two pieces.

The Options for Freeing Up Time chart (see Image #5 in the Appendix) can serve as a tool to help you strike the right balance while also helping yourself and your company maximize R.O.T—by determining which responsibilities can be handled more effectively in another way.

This includes determining if there's a role that you or the entire company should simply stop doing (Column One). You may identify certain tasks that over time have come to deliver little intrinsic value to your business and your customers.

Column Two notes which responsibilities make sense to outsource to business partners or contractors. They usually are activities that are not your core competencies; those activities that you do not do well and/or that do not provide you with any strategic advantage. For these activities, a strategic partner may be able to not only handle the basics, but may also be able to provide strategic ideas that you can leverage. Often the strategic ideas are something you would not get by hiring a lower-level employee to cover these duties, such as finance/accounting, human resources and marketing.

Column Three tasks are the things you can delegate to others in the company. In addition to allowing you to focus on more strategic initiatives, you also give others the opportunity to advance their knowledge, value and careers by assigning them something that will help them grow their capabilities.

Column Four identifies responsibilities and tasks that can be automated through hardware and software systems that reduce the amount of manual intervention time. Here's where you can improve the R.O.T of your entire company.

Examples of how some Leaders Recharge Their Batteries

- Take a two-day retreat every quarter away from the office; give your employees a form ahead of time to fill out in order to identify the things they would like you to consider.
- Spend two afternoons per month at an off-site office; this takes you away from your normal distractions while also giving you the opportunity to reconnect with others in the company.

- Stay at work late one designated night per week; this helps your family know what your schedule will be and allows you to get more work done.
- Allocate exercise time for yourself; one of my clients, who works many evenings, started doing yoga three mornings per week and now comes into the office later each day to give herself more energy.
- Consider taking an entire month off each year to fully recharge your batteries and give yourself ample time to decompress; this helps focus on strategy planning with renewed vigor.
- Combine recreation—golf, skiing and other physical activities—with client/prospect meetings during the business week.
- Take every Wednesday afternoon off—it's a great mid-week rejuvenation tactic.
- Schedule long weekend get-aways with your spouse, family or friends once per month

By Avoiding Distractions, You *Can* Make a Change

People who struggle in their effort to maximize their Return-On-Time usually do so because they are distracted by the factors discussed above—the rapid pace of change, too much accessibility given to others, digital overload, and the "Badge of Being Busy." They take it as a given that things cannot change. Their cell phones have to be on all the time, and they need to be accessible to their staff 24x7—because that's what good leaders do.

Don't take these things as a given. You *can* make changes. First commit *to wanting to improve* and then change your priorities. Give yourself permission to explore your inner thoughts so you don't keep yourself in the dark as to what you truly want. Reflect more often and immediately follow the Reflect step with the Plan and Do steps. A mediocre plan put into action always beats a "perfect" plan that stays on the shelf because you keep trying to improve it.

Along the way, celebrate your milestone achievements and give yourself quiet time to restore your energy. As noted at the beginning of this chapter, if you don't prioritize your time, someone else will.

Life is short: You deserve to maximize your R.O.T—*for the relatively short time we are on this earth.*

Chapter 6: Change Your Environments

- Are you living to work or are you working to live?

- Does your career serve your personal life and vice versa?

- Are you living where you want to? If not, where is your ultimate place to live?

- Are you playing a key role within all the social groups you belong to?

- Have you discussed with the important people in your life where you want to live and how you want your social groups to change?

All of these questions relate to assessing the many environments of your life in which you live and work. They include physical locations—such as your home and place of business—as well as the several social environments in which we all live and work. Environments exist in your relationship with your significant other and with your family and friends. Social environments also include the business groups and recreational groups you belong to. Another environment to consider is your community—at the local, state and even the national level.

Some environments exist for many years, while others such as social/community groups, might exist for short periods of time. In all cases, it's best to be in environments where trust exists among all the members.

Over time, it's important to periodically assess each environment and determine if changes are needed or if things can stay the way they are. In some cases, you may decide it's time to exit an environment, which may mean a physical move but could also mean leaving a relationship you have with a person or a group.

Many people feel as though they are stuck in their environments and cannot effect any changes. But you may very well be able to influence more than you think. If you get creative and give it a try—while also communicating to others in that environment with the right intentions—you can often make a positive impact on yourself and others.

For some environments, you may decide to put up with conditions you don't like for a limited amount of time. Just knowing that you have a plan for how things will change down the road can often be enough to get you through the interim. Talk things through with the others who are involved and realize...things can change!

Remove the Regret of Failing to Try

A woman I know and respect, who has always believed in family first and being thrifty, told her three children as they graduated from high school that there was no need to add expensive travel to their college costs. So she required all of them to go to a college within a few hours' drive.

At the time, I thought this was rather restrictive. But now, I'm envious! Her children all stayed in New England and married people from New England, so the grandchildren are close to her as well.

Whether the approach she took is right or wrong is subjective; many people come down on both sides, and it's sometimes a matter of life's circumstance for each family. But this is also an example of proactively acting upon your environment—as opposed to just assuming something is a given.

If you approach people that you share an environment with in the right way, you can at least try to see if something can be set up the way you like. You won't be able to influence all your environments as she was able to in this case, and you may have to accept other people's preferences. But you can at least remove the regret of never having given it a try.

Make an Impact on Temporary Environments

Some of your environments may exist for a very short time, but you can still have an impact if you choose to get involved. I used to be much more of an introvert and often did not step up in environments where I felt something was wrong. I just tried to get along in corporate America. But now I believe every environment belongs to everyone that's involved.

As an example, I once attended a dinner with about 500 people that was hosted by a major newspaper. The guest speaker was a reporter who had just risked his life spending a month in the Middle East to write about US efforts to establish peace. The room was packed, and the newspaper was treating us to a food and drinks. When the CEO introduced the reporter, the room was so loud that no one could hear her. Even when the reporter started to speak, the room was still too loud.

I had enough at that point…I yelped and then hollered loudly, "Let's Have a Little Class!"

The room immediately fell silent. Looking back, I could not believe I had the courage to do that. But the CEO, the reporter and many others thanked me. Now if I don't step up, I get mad at myself. The environment belongs to Us, and we all have a right to make the environment work well!

If you don't like one of your environments, proactively modify it. When you do so in the right way, you can make changes, and people will respect you even more. Tell them you want the environment to succeed, but also tell them when you see something you think can improve.

At the same time, don't judge—be aware of the context but also have courage to state how you feel. I call this having "fierce conversations in a non-judgmental way." Seek first to understand then be understood, and turn to an assertive learning mode so that you don't shy away. By taking this approach, you can learn how things feel to others and communicate how things feel to you.

How to Assess Your Environments

A number of my clients—especially ones who work for large companies and spend a lot of time working away from Maine—say they don't feel connected to their family or town, and that feeling connected is a driving factor of happiness. They might also say they don't have any real friends because they are so busy leading their company, taking care of their children or parents, or serving on boards. The last thing on their priority list is developing and maintaining personal relationships.

Perhaps the best approach in this case is to simply start by being aware and considering the possibilities of how you might change your environments. Take a look and decide which parts work for you and which do not. You will often discover ways to balance the amount of time you spend so that you flourish and enjoy each environment to a much greater extent.

As you consider changes you might want to make, assess your emotional environments at home, at work and other places you spend time:

- What kind of emotional environment do you want to be in?
- What's the degree of trust, gratitude and dependability of each environment?
- Whether it's a board, a community or a neighborhood, how does the group handle problems?
- When problems occur, does the group overreact or are they calm and thoughtful?
- Do they seek to first understand versus placing blame?
- Do they involve all the appropriate people in addressing problems?

For any environment you are in—these elements either are present...or they are not present. Many people sit on the sidelines and just complain, but you have the power to step up and make changes.

Tips for Changing Your Environments

As pointed out above, your environments include where you live and work physically as well as the social groups you are part of—family, friends, the business and the community. Consider what is best for you in all these circumstances and periodically analyze what you want to change:

- What do you like about the group?
- How can you attempt to improve the group?
- Should you exit the group?
- Is there a "fierce" conversation you need to have with a fellow member? (see Chapter 5)

For the places you live and work...

- Which physical aspects work well?
- Which aspects don't work well?

- Do any aspects impact your productivity, either positively or negatively?
- Which aspects impact your mojo or your happiness?

As you identify the things that annoy you (perhaps the neighbors!), put them into context among all the aspects that please you. Analyze what you have; this will help you determine what you want to work towards.

You may discover it's worth living with a couple annoyances, or maybe you will decide to try to change them. Instead of moving, minor adjustments might save you a lot of trouble.

When my wife and I started to get bored with the layout of our house, we took down one of the internal walls, and it opened the view within the house dramatically. I could see all the way through the house from my office and up the street, so I knew when our sons were coming home. Just that little change gave me an extra jolt of joy each day and a whole new perspective about my physical environment!

A few years later, as my wife and I considered downsizing our home, we found the ideal condo and immediately fell in love with it. But after considering it was 15 miles further from my base of clients, I realized it would cost me about 100 hours in travel each year vs. time that could be spent collaborating with clients or enjoying fun experiences. My wife's commute would also have been similarly impacted. We thus decided to add a proximity limitation to our condo wish list.

Before Changing One of Your Environments
If you decide to change one of your environments, take a good look at the new environment you plan to transition to—making sure it truly offers the changes you seek. For example, if moving from a city to the country, consider the travel stress if it takes you further away from your job and hobbies. Most environment changes, such as buying a

new home, have multiple factors to consider. Moving to an older home may reduce your mortgage payments but could also increase your maintenance costs.

Money is often the prime factor in driving people to want to live and work in different environments. The desire to change can also be related to self-worth, self-image and personal wants.

As an example, growing up in the middle class in Maine, I saw people who came to our town (Kennebunk) for the summer and was envious of how they could afford to spend their time golfing, on the water, and dining at fine restaurants. These feelings became a driving force early in my professional career when I moved my family from Maine to Ohio. I did not want to live in Ohio, but that's where my company wanted me to go, and I felt compelled by the need to earn more money and provide for my family.

Later in life, the drive for money lessened in importance and gave way to a greater focus on my family. My wife and I realized our parents were growing older, and our sons did not know their extended family very well. We knew we would regret it if we stayed in Ohio, so we moved back to Maine.

This change in my environment also got my creative juices flowing and allowed me to flourish in my new career as a business coach—and still earn the money I needed to sustain my family in a business environment that was also much better for me. This is a prime example of how changing one environment that's particularly bothersome can open a whole new world of possibilities in another environment.

Suggestions for Connecting with Your Environments

As you have noticed throughout each chapter of this book, I provide personal experiences and suggestions based on things that have worked well for me. I do so in the hopes that you can relate my personal experiences to something personal in your life, and perhaps make the changes you need for a better life and work environment.

Here are several of my experiences when it comes to changing the environments in which I have lived and worked. I hope you can find one or two that resonate with you so you can be courteously bold about making changes:

- **Be a Professional Friend**: My role as a business coach has a great impact on my friend environment, expanding it through those I collaborate with on a professional basis. When consulting with my clients and hearing about one of their personal challenges, I try to go beyond sympathizing with them by offering advice. I don't push things, I simply suggest ideas. When possible, I also try to be a professional friend to those I meet outside of work—looking for suggestions that can help them with their professional careers and their personal happiness.

- **Connect with Many Environments**: I try to be relevant and have an impact on all my environments; this means connecting and staying connected, whether it's the people I coach, my town, the state, or the business community. By accepting an invitation to be a guest columnist for a business publication, my columns appear on a regular basis, so business leaders across the state can get to know me and reflect on my ideas and learnings.

- **Market Yourself**: I like to be around vibrant people who practice the three P's: Principled, Personable and Progressive. So for both business and personal relationships, I try to be where there are people that I want to be with. This means finding the events they go to, and putting myself out there while prepping with a couple questions in order to get people engaged. I try to uncover hobbies and other interests that help strike up conversations about common interests as I attend various business group events—knowing that's where my prospects like to go as well. I also proactively seek speaking opportunities. They are a great way to connect with many people all at once and to market my skills.

- **Give Yourself Permission to Enjoy**: Knowing that active people like to be around active people, I "gave myself permission" to join a golf country club to socialize as my sons went off to college and to build business relationships with clients and prospects. Many of my clients ski in the winter, so I also gave myself permission to take a weekday each month to invite three clients to ski.

- **Get Involved in the Community**: I accepted an offer to be the ambassador for my city's business association. They liked that I was welcoming and inclusive, and that I would meet with new business people who had just moved to town. At the state level, I joined the advisory board for the business school that I attended. These groups help me give back and provide satisfaction that I can have an impact on the environments that I am part of.

My Personal Validation Moments
The relationships you build with people by practicing habits such as these will sometimes amaze you. Because of the efforts I've made to connect with each of my social environments, I've been very fortunate to find myself in some truly spiritual moments that seem to transcend the importance and value of forming special relationships with a variety of people:

- A fairly short time after joining a regularly scheduled golfing foursome with three people that I had just met, I was with them when I found out my father had passed away. But the connection we established by playing golf together on a regular basis was already strong. They helped me get back home on what was a long car drive, and they even attended my father's funeral.

- One of my clients, who I knew very well, did not find out about my father's passing until the morning of the funeral, but he still cleared his schedule to come. And when attending the funeral of another client, his son, who I also knew, told me what a good friend I was to his father.

- Another client called me and told me he considers me one of his top five best friends. That gave me a very warm, satisfying feeling. But he was also calling to tell me he had leukemia. This was a sad day, but it meant a lot to me that I meant that much to him.

When you mix your outdoor environment—even if it's only temporary—with your personal relationships, you can truly bring yourself to feeling as though you are on hallowed ground:

- When I attended a sunrise service on Sugarloaf Mountain for an Easter Sunrise Service, and sang Amazing Grace as we watched the sun come up, touching the United States for the very first time that day. This experience brought me to tears; I was truly home!

- One of the things they say every Mainer must do is climb Mt. Katahdin—the tallest in the state. I did so with five friends, and we took a picture at the top that we all treasure today. I also experienced another Maine must do—kayaking down the Allagash River—with my father and sister when I was 14. When you experience great moments with the people you cherish, it makes the experience so much more rewarding.

- I signed my first client as a business coach while I was living in Maine, but my immediate family had not yet moved from Ohio. I thus celebrated by drinking champagne with my parents. The conversation quickly turned into an apology that I had lived so far away for so long. But my parents were just happy that I was back and doing something I enjoyed. That helped me let go of a lot of the guilty feelings I was storing up inside. A few years later, after we had all moved to Maine and when my mother's health began to fail, she said, "Having you here in Maine is the best medicine." A few years after that, as my father reached his later stages of life, he said "Slap me if I panic!" He was a very stoic, self-reliant and intelligent person, but this was his way of saying, son, "I now need and want your help." Both of these interactions show how our roles of life can be reversed. In both cases, I was glad I could be with my parents during their last several years and help them out.

- Combining work with family, I once took my parents with me to Miami for a business conference. During the days, I got the work done that I needed to at the conference while my parents enjoyed the Florida sun. At night, we enjoyed dinner and the city together.

- With my wife, sons and future daughter-in-law, we spent time at a lakefront home in Bridgton, Maine that we rented from my childhood music teacher. We enjoyed a view of Pleasant Mountain where I had skied with my sons and earned my Boy Scout Merit Badge with my dad. Simply sitting on the dock with my family near the calm water while all those memories flowed through my thoughts was a very "meant-to-be moment."

Begin Your Own Assessments—and Surprise Yourself!
When people care for you, it's truly touching and turns your environments into special places—you can't beat that kind of validation. You may experience other successes, but if you don't foster environments where you make genuine personal connections, you will not feel fulfilled.

To increase your impact on your environments, begin to regularly assess all your physical and emotional environments on at least an annual basis. And don't be afraid to ask the tough questions of those you share environments with as you strive to make things better.

You just might surprise yourself at how much of an effect you can have and how much you can make your environments better for yourself and those you care about most.

Chapter 7: Manage Your Attitude Towards Money

After managing yourself and your relationships, improving how well you manage your money is likely high on your priority list. But for many people, managing money is a major struggle.

If this is true for you, here's a suggestion for how to attack the problem. Before trying to improve how well you manage money, focus first on managing your *attitude* towards money. Once you gain the right perspective, the task of managing your money so you can prosper becomes a lot easier.

As you work to modify your attitude, keep these five objectives in mind:

1. Don't rely on money as your primary measure of success and happiness.
2. Realize the lack of enough money to survive *can be* a source of unhappiness.
3. Avoid thinking of money as evil, and avoid feeling negative toward those who have more money than you.
4. Actively manage your finances on a regular basis.
5. Discuss finances with the important people in your life.

As you work your way through these objectives, concentrate on managing your own situation and avoid feeling jealous about the finances of those around you. Any jealousies you feel will likely negatively impact how you present yourself and how you register with others. Also be purposeful in the presentation of yourself. It's OK to do what comes natural, but be aware of what you project to others by the choices you make in how you spend your money.

Don't rely on money as your primary measure of success and happiness

The important things in life are not actual things—all the stuff that money can buy. While money provides flexibility in what you can and can't do, the things you buy aren't what make you happy. Your relationships with yourself and others truly drive fulfillment and happiness.

A study from a few years ago—by Dr. Daniel Kahneman and Dr. Angus Deaton from the Center for Health and Wellbeing at Princeton University—tried to correlate money and happiness. The two doctors found there was some level of income ($75K as of the date of the study) where people who made less than that amount were less happy. However, those who made more than the $75K were not necessarily more happy.[1]

People do need to attain some level of income to make money a non-issue and bring financial serenity into their lives. It's vital to determine for yourself what that level is so you can make money a non-issue—either you have enough now or you have a plan to generate enough in the future so you can focus on the important things of life.

No doubt, it can be hard to set aside the effects that not having enough money has on your ego, your self-image and your pride. To one extent or another, we all try to "keep up with the Joneses" of the world. Some people actually turn it into an obsessive competition where they keep score of who has the best house, the best car and other material items.

This can manifest itself in people overspending on major purchases that bring them into debt. Or they may opt for the relatively cheap "retail therapy" approach, such as overspending on clothing (one of my tendencies that I have to watch). They do so while forsaking other areas of their financial life—they either want the ultimate house, car or clothes, and they get trapped in a never ending cycle and forgo more important financial serenity goals.

Owning the best house in a certain neighborhood or the hottest sports car might be their definition of happiness. But being "house poor" or "car poor" usually creates stress in other areas. That's because people who overspend in one area usually don't create long-term goals. They need to experience immediate self-satisfaction when interacting with people by showing off their expensive stuff.

Consider the case of Tony Manero (played by John Travolta) in the movie *Saturday Night Fever*. He worked in a paint store and lived with his parents. But he sure did spend a lot of money on clothes so he could dress to the nines when went out to the discos!

Seeking instant gratification like this can alleviate immediate shortcomings, but it comes at the expense of long-term needs. Some people who lease cars, for example, drive more car than they can afford. Or they may owe more than the car is worth. On the other end of the spectrum, Sam Walton—the founder of Walmart and Sam's Club stores, who at the time of his death in 1992 had achieved a net worth of billions of dollars, drove an antique red truck. My belief is that there is nothing wrong with driving a nice vehicle; just be aware of how much of your self-image is connected to it.

For most, it's best to find a happy medium between saving for the future and rewarding yourself today. One of my clients was averse to spending money on himself but was overly generous to others. He finally consulted with a financial planner and found a way for him and his wife to go on one big trip each year with one of their three adult children, each taking a turn every third year. My client essentially balanced the immediate desire to travel with spending time with his children, but not overdoing it so much that he could not still save for the future.

Realize the lack of enough money to survive can be a source of unhappiness

While excessive money does not guarantee happiness, a lack of money can cause unhappiness, as referenced in the study cited above. This is true for individuals as well as couples—unhappiness caused by a lack of money or other financial mistrust is the most common factor in divorces. This is not to say by any means that those who lack money are unhappy. Many people with next to nothing find great happiness in the other areas of their lives.

If you are fortunate enough to come into a lot of money, it's critical to manage it because losing money can be a lot more detrimental than never having money in the first place. Many lottery winners often go bankrupt and wish they had never won. They assumed they had unlimited funds, and with many of their friends and relatives begging for money, they found it difficult to maintain their relationships. Some winners end up moving and having to look for a whole new set of friends.

To avoid unhappiness from the result of not having enough money, the first key is to develop and stick to a well-planned budget. Measure what you earn and spend today. Then determine what you are capable of earning and by how much you can reduce your spending so that you set aside enough to save for the future. 10% is a good savings goal to shoot for, but it's OK to start small and work your way up, even if today you can only set aside 1%.

By monitoring your money situation frequently, you will find your ability to manage your money will increase tremendously. It's that age-old saying, "That which gets monitored and measured gets managed!"

Remember to also consider the revenue side and don't under-value your ability to generate a higher income. Getting to the point where you productively manage your finances will take time. But if you move in the right direction, you can avoid unhappy feelings.

Avoid thinking of money as evil, and avoid feeling negative toward those who have more money than you

This attribute about your attitude towards money is a two-way street: It includes both the way you view other people with money and how you feel about the way people view your approach towards money. It's easy to be influenced negatively by either aspect.

Some people seem afraid to earn a lot of money because they don't feel worthy, or they think they can't do so legitimately. They automatically push back on the concept of achieving wealth. But there's nothing wrong with making a lot of money (whatever the definition of that is to you).

Many people without money also tend to think that money is evil. Consider all the political ads that blame the economy's woes on Wall Street millionaires. They think wealthy people must have cheated someone, had money given to them, or lucked into money. They despise other people who flash their houses, their cars or their clothing. They have an ingrained bias and assumptions that "those people must be up to no good!"

Avoid categorizing people just because they have money. I have met millionaires who would help anyone and give the shirts off their backs.

I've also met poor people who would steal the shirt off your back. There's no correlation between having money and the quality of human beings.

The presupposition that money is evil often comes down to jealousy, and sometimes that jealousy is pointed at something really small. I was once criticized by a friend for the shoes I was wearing, feeling as though it was another example of me trying to look like the better man.

Those who have earned money have also earned the right to enjoy the stuff their money can buy. But at the same time, be conscious of whether anything you buy might be a way of bragging about the money you have earned. You don't need to apologize for your success, and you have the right to enjoy what you have earned, but see if you can find a balance somewhere in between.

From the business perspective, some businesses are fearful of charging too much for their products and services. They could actually generate more profit by charging prices that are relative to a product's value to the customer vs. its cost to produce. In many cases, people and businesses are willing to pay a price that makes sense relative to the great value that they achieve from superior products and services.

One of the business leaders I coached would quite often be asked to put extensive accessories on new boats, such as adding $100K worth of electronics to a $500K boat. His employees would frequently discount the work since it seemed like so much money to them. It's important to feel comfortable with a real definition of your own value and the value of your products and services. Charging more does not make you evil—there's no reason you can't make a reasonable profit. Profits allow you to develop more solutions for your customers, create more jobs, and increase the stability of the business so you can keep serving your customers.

By coming to grips with your beliefs about other peoples' money and your own money, you can elevate your own value and avoid feeling envious towards others. Removing that envy will also allow you to build stronger relationships with those people, who in turn may end up playing an important role in the monetary value of your personal and/or your business lives.

Don't be afraid to try being the "the nicest rich person" anyone ever met. You can be both!

Actively manage your finances on a regular basis

To paraphrase a quote heard by one of my clients in a seminar with Warren Buffet, "if you remember nothing else, spend less than you make."

The concept seems so simple but many people make the mistake of anticipating they will have more money to spend later on and thus do not contribute regularly to their savings. That's why it's important to develop a flexible plan for managing your money that functions effectively during the different phases of life.

A flexible plan helps you avoid overspending when earning less than your predicted income for a period of time. An effective plan also helps you avoid spending money on things you don't really need when extra, unplanned income comes in. Review your financial management plan at least annually but preferably quarterly or even monthly. Also reevaluate when any major financial events occur that create big drops or increases in revenue or costs.

The ultimate goal should be financial serenity—where you have enough and don't worry about money too much of the time. To succeed, most people require some training, whether it's from a financial planner or by reading up on the various ways to create and stick to a budget. There are also various tracking tools that can provide a big assist.

If you can't turn to a professional or spend money on financial planning software, consider working with a personal friend or family member, and don't forget the old-school approach of paper and pencil! Just getting something down in writing with a budget for spending in various areas and then setting savings goals can be enough to get your momentum going in the right direction.

Be sure to pay yourself first, and as suggested above, try to allocate 10% of every dollar you earn towards your retirement savings. If you are fortunate enough to work for a company with a matching 401K plan, then that will help even more!

Amazingly, not enough people take advantage of such programs. Many employers are willing to literally double your investment, and the amount employees invest is tax free until withdrawn in retirement—when their tax rate will be much lower. Who can beat that!

But also plan for an occasional splurge for fun. A good example is one of my sons and his summer jobs during high school and college. He would set a savings goal at the beginning of each summer but also plan a big-item purchase to reward himself at end of each summer.

Long-term money goals to consider include determining the income level you need to *survive* and to maintain your standard of living when you retire. Then determine the income level you will need to *thrive* and to do the things on your bucket list. The amounts you target may change over time, so keep assessing your situation. If you determine that saving enough to provide you with a $4K per month income might cover your living expenses while saving enough to provide a $5K per month income would allow you to take a trip each year, you just might motivate yourself to decrease your spending or increase your revenue.

The payoff is that you will have goals to work towards rather than going along blindly and assuming you will be OK. Even if you are making sufficient money, you need goals to protect yourself from taking too much of a risk.

Discuss finances with the important people in your life

Failure to discuss your finances with your significant others—whether it's a marriage or a business partnership—can often lead to the break-up of the relationship. In many cases, one person takes care of everything and allows the other person to stay in the dark. If there's a sudden misfortune in finances, a misunderstanding due to the information that was not shared could lead to a complete breakdown in the relationship. And if one person in the partnership suddenly leaves—due to a death or other life-altering event—the other person may be left trying to manage finances for which they have no information and/or skills. You don't want to leave your significant other to the mercy of others.

To avoid this situation, regularly discuss finances with your significant others. Set budgets and goals together including the regular fixed expense budget and putting away an emergency budget for unplanned expenses. Also keep records of important information that both of you have access to such as account numbers and the contact info of mentors, coaches and anyone else with fiduciary responsibilities. Any advisors you use should know both of you and the other key people in your lives, such as parents and children, or senior executives in a business situation.

As you create and manage your own budget, take the opportunity to also teach your children how to manage the costs of their lives. If helping a child through college, create a spreadsheet that breaks down their costs vs. your costs. Also discuss the consequences of student loans and who has long-term responsibility to pay them off.

As your parents age, they too will likely need your help with their budgets, particularly if they are unaware of changing costs while on a fixed income. It's good to plan ahead, such as adding your name to their bank accounts, which makes the role of Executor easier when it comes time. Older parents often need help when it comes to other financial matters such as selling their home. I was lucky enough that my father recognized when he had reached the stage where he needed help. He realized he might not be fully aware of the things he needed to know and was ready to turn to me for assistance.

This same concept can be very powerful in business. Leaders often say they want their employees to think like them and be very mindful of how they spend the company's money. Seldom however, do leaders take the time to educate their employees about the basics of the financial aspects of the business. If a leader can simplify what happens to a dollar that comes into the business, such as the percentage that goes to fixed and variable expenses, employees can begin providing valuable ideas about how to reduce expenses and increase revenues.

Fierce Conversations—with Yourself and Others

Although the concepts put forth in this chapter seem relatively simple, they can be much easier said than done for many people. When it comes to managing money, you need to commit to having "fierce conversations" (as discussed in Chapter 5) with yourself and the important people in your life so that you can develop the right attitude towards money.

It will take courage to cut your spending. It will take discipline to pay yourself first. And when discussing what expenses to take away or reduce with someone you love or do business with, the conversation could get tense.

But if you don't solve the challenge of achieving financial serenity, you will constantly feel something nagging at your conscience. You may be able to avoid that inner voice for a few years, but eventually, the lack of a plan will cause heartache and unnecessary distress.

Start changing your attitude towards money today—so you can create a financial plan that enables you to both have fun and save for the future. You *can* attain the best of both worlds!

---

1. "High income improves evaluation of life but not emotional well-being," by Daniel Kahneman and Angus Deaton, Center for Health and Well-being, Princeton University, August 4, 2010: https://www.princeton.edu/~deaton/downloads/deaton_kahneman_high_income_improves_evaluation_August2010.pdf

Chapter 8: Putting It All Together

The lessons and advice presented in this book are not intended to get you to a specific destination in your personal life and professional life; They are tactics for enjoying your journey by being intentional and living life your way, and to help you define your own version of fulfillment and happiness.

Fulfillment and happiness require you to continue to follow the process of Plan>>Do>>Learn>>Adjust as you achieve your goals in each of the eight steps of your own personal journey:

The Eight Steps of Your Personal Journey

1. Own Responsibility for Your Happiness—the first step to live your life the way you are meant to, and to enable all the steps that follow.
2. Lead Your Personal Growth—be intentional and lead the way on a regular basis.
3. Deepen Your Important Relationships—the key to ultimate happiness.
4. Commit to Achieving Meaningful Goals—go beyond just creating to actually doing.
5. Feed Your Mojo—by managing your energy and focus.
6. Be a Time Leader—maximize your Return-On-Time and set an example for others.
7. Create and Modify Your Physical and Social Environments—to sync with your personal rhythms.
8. Achieve Financial Serenity—to help you focus more energy on all the preceding steps.

Within each of the previous chapters, we delved into some of the tools you can use for each step. Here's a rundown for quick reference as you strive for success in each area:

Own Responsibility for Your Happiness—Before you can feel happy about your present and optimistic about your future, it's important to achieve closure on any past issues, frustrations or disappointments. Let go of your excuses for not achieving things you wanted in the past, and don't allow yourself to be held back by what someone either did to you or didn't do for you.

As you look forward, avoid enabling others to dictate how you feel about yourself. This will give you the freedom to envision your perfect future. Start by brainstorming and just write down what comes to mind. Let yourself dream and don't hold back—otherwise it's too hard to start. As you envision the dream, it will eventually come into focus. You can then define the steps for achieving that vision.

Lead Your Personal Growth—Find the courage to look yourself in the mirror on a regular basis. And don't wait until something goes wrong. Make it a regular habit!

At the same time, seek feedback from others to see how you appear from the outside. After factoring your viewpoint with the viewpoints of others, define the improvements you want to make and then ask for help on what you can do to improve. Consider working with an accountability partner. This step works better when you help someone else and offer each other kudos and constructive criticism.

Deepen Your Important Relationships—A key aspect to this step is to prioritize your relationships to make sure you focus on those that are most important. You can't form deep relationships with everyone, and depending on your needs, you may only want to establish strong relationships with just a few people.

Consider your significant other, your children, your parents, your siblings and your close friends. You may not be able, or you may not want to go deep with everyone. And who you choose to get closer to may change over time.

As you interact with those important to you, be authentic, and express your appreciation—tell them what they mean to you. At the same time, admit any mistakes you made in the past and eliminate any regrets about someone you did not thank or to whom you need to express your apologies—before your relationship grows too distant or you lose your chance forever.

Commit to Achieving Meaningful Goals—For those who find setting and achieving goals to be too much of a struggle, it's often because they don't first consider *why* they want to achieve something and *why* they want to make a positive impact on their own life, the lives of those important to them, and their businesses.

Why you choose to do something is actually more important than what you choose to do. The *why* puts passion behind your efforts, and that passion will not only drive you in achieving meaningful goals, but also attract others to you—whether it's for forming a personal relationship or doing business. After determining the *why* behind each of your goals and what motivates you, make sure each goal is stated clearly and meaningfully. Goals often come down to what you want people to say about you when you're gone.

Make your goals SMART—Specific, Measurable, Actionable, Realistic and Time-Bound. Declaring your goals to yourself and others will add even more passion, so gain consensus with key stakeholders in your life who are impacted by your goals. Define the first step for each goal and each subsequent step as best you can. You likely won't know all the steps at the beginning, but you can usually define the first couple steps and then go from there. Once you succeed with step one and step two, creating step three and step four is usually easier.

Also be sure to track your progress and reassess where you're at on a regular basis. Given what you learn along the way, you may change your approach and/or your goals. You may also discover that your *why* has changed.

Feed Your Mojo—Success in all of these steps requires mojo—a zest for life and the feeling of adrenaline running through your veins for what you are trying to accomplish. To feed your mojo, identify the people as well as your various roles and other things that give you energy. Also identify those people, those roles and other things that drain your energy.

Then determine why certain people and things give or take away your energy. This will help you make sure you adjust your activities so you can plug into good mojo sources more often and avoid the bad sources when possible. For some relationships and roles, you may discover you only need to adjust one component to increase your mojo or decrease the impact of any mojo drains. Be sure to do more of the first and less of the latter!

Be a Time Leader—Following closely on the step of feeding your mojo, define the best uses of your time based on what feeds your mojo in each of your social and physical environments. One way to elevate your Return-On-Time and to set an example for others is to bring other leaders together who are easy to be with and fun to go places with. Working as a group, you can help each other define your own versions of success and happiness. Through any self-examination you share with each other, all of you can enjoy the journey and learn to not be too hard on yourself.

As you discover what are you are good at, you can then progress your work life from a job to a career and then to a passionate calling. In parallel, you can also progress your personal life to include deeper relationships. As you experience both journeys, you will realize just how much your work life and your personal life integrate with each other.

Create and Modify Your Physical and Social Environments—As you consider all the social and physical environments you interact with, strive to make your work life serve your personal life (rather than vice-versa) and seek ways to integrate your personal life with your work. Perhaps you can travel to places you want to visit while you also work. Or perhaps the people you work and collaborate with can also become your friends. Your friends might even be able to play a key role in your work life.

Know too that you contribute—positively or negatively—to all of your environments. You can choose to affect change where you live and where you work as well as the social groups you belong to including family, professional groups, your community, your state, the country and even the world. Adapt each of your environments to be conducive with feeding your mojo.

Achieve Financial Serenity—Those who do not achieve financial serenity often find it difficult to succeed in the other seven steps. What we have for wealth in the future to live on and what we can pass along to our children can weigh heavily on many of us and distract us from achieving success in other areas.

Financial serenity is not about wanting and needing more. It's not your major source of happiness. Financial serenity comes from managing your attitude towards money. It means striving to spend less than you make, paying yourself first, and managing your risks and your investments.

Set your financial goals with your significant other to avoid future misunderstandings and missed expectations. Also remember to define financial rewards so you can enjoy what you have earned while being reasonably frugal. We all deserve to have fun along the way!

What Comes Next?

As you achieve success in any or all of these areas, you can then set new goals that bring you even more happiness, a greater sense of achievement and most importantly—deeper relationships with those people who are most important to you.

It's Launch Time!

How many coaches does it take to change a light bulb? Just one! But the light bulb really has to want to change!

Within this book, you now have access to many tools and processes to get yourself going in the right direction to achieve more fulfillment in your personal and business lives. I urge you to not settle for mediocrity and feel as though that's good enough—claiming to be happy to others when you are not really happy inside yourself. Reach for more and take the risk that you and your relationships can improve!

I also hope the concepts presented in this book have been inspirational. Whether you achieve improvement in just one area, or if you find success sometime down the road, the key is to just keep trying. You don't need to progress in all eight areas—pick one that either excites or bothers you the most, and focus your efforts there.

Improvement in one area will likely spawn improvement in a second area and so on.

Look towards the end—your retirement: How long will you work? What do you want retirement to look like? Maybe you will adjust and shift into retirement gradually rather than stopping work all at once. Cold stops can be difficult, so it's better to gear up for doing other things as you wind down your work life.

There are no specific timelines you need to adhere to and it's never too late to start. While those who begin working towards retirement earlier in life generally find the road easier to travel, it's certainly within everyone's means to jump on the road to retirement later in life and still find a way to succeed.

Those with persistent effort toward clear goals tend to eventually achieve success. What you have achieved to this point in your life and your current state of happiness are not nearly as important as the journey ahead that you envision. Going in the right direction holds far more value than how far you have traveled.

Enjoy the journey ahead—be kind and be joyful—and may the wind be at your back!

Image #1 Career Opportunity Prioritization Analysis

Attribute Career Type / Opportunity	Attribute 1	Attribute 2	Attribute 3	Attribute 4	Attribute 5	Attribute 6	Total
Career 1	5	1	3	1	5	3	18
Career 2	1	3	5	5	1	5	20
Career 3	3	3	1	1	3	1	12
Career 4	3	1	1	3	3	3	14
Career 5	1	5	3	1	3	1	14
Opportunity 1	1	3	3	1	3	3	14
Opportunity 2	3	3	1	3	1	1	12
Opportunity 3	5	1	3	5	1	3	18
Opportunity 4	3	3	5	3	5	5	24
Opportunity 5	3	1	1	3	1	1	10

Instructions:

1. Identify all the different careers/jobs you have held. These can be limited to the most recent, or you may go back to the very first job you held as a teenager or even a "job" you held growing up, such as fundraising for a group you belonged to.
2. Identify six attributes you want to find in your next career/job opportunity.
3. Fill in the matrix as to how well each of your past careers/jobs fulfilled those attributes—see the scoring key below.
4. Looking at the total scores, compare past career/job experiences to identify those that fulfilled your attributes the most; this may help you identify new opportunities to pursue.
5. Fill in the matrix as to how well each potential new opportunity will fulfill those attributes using the same scoring key.
6. Looking at the total scores, compare how well each future opportunity fulfills the attributes you seek to determine which opportunity you will pursue.

Past Career/Future Opportunity Scoring Key

1 = Opportunity meets/satisfies this attribute significantly less than others
3 = Opportunity meets/satisfies this attribute about the same as others
5 = Opportunity meets/satisfies this attribute significantly more than others

Image #2: The Wheel of Life

The eight sections in the Wheel of Life, as drawn below, represent balance among the key areas of life. Using the center of the wheel as a rating of 0, and the outer edge as a rating of 10, rank your level of satisfaction with each life area by drawing a curved line to create a new outer edge. This new edge will demonstrate how well-balanced your life is.

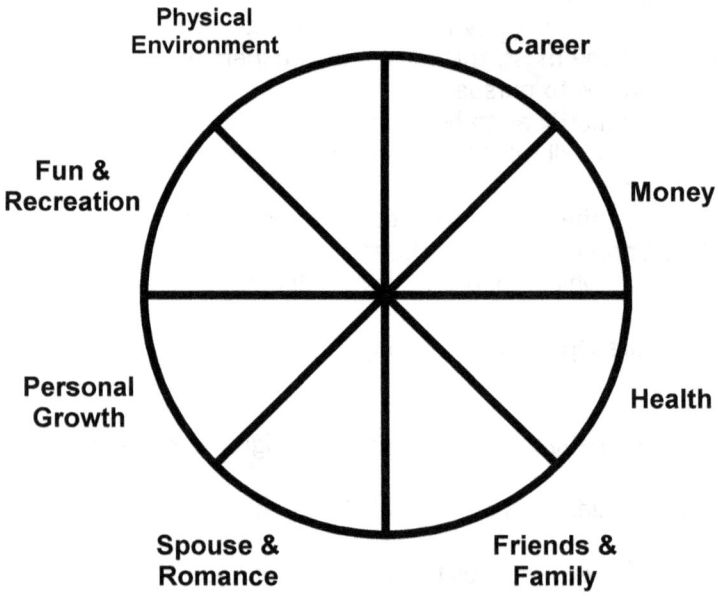

Image #3: The Wheel of Business

The eight sections in the Wheel of Business, as drawn below, represent perfect balance among the main components of business operations. Using the center of the wheel as a rating of 0, and the outer edge as a rating of 10, rank your level of satisfaction with each business area by drawing a curved line to create a new outer edge. This edge will demonstrate how well-balanced your business is.

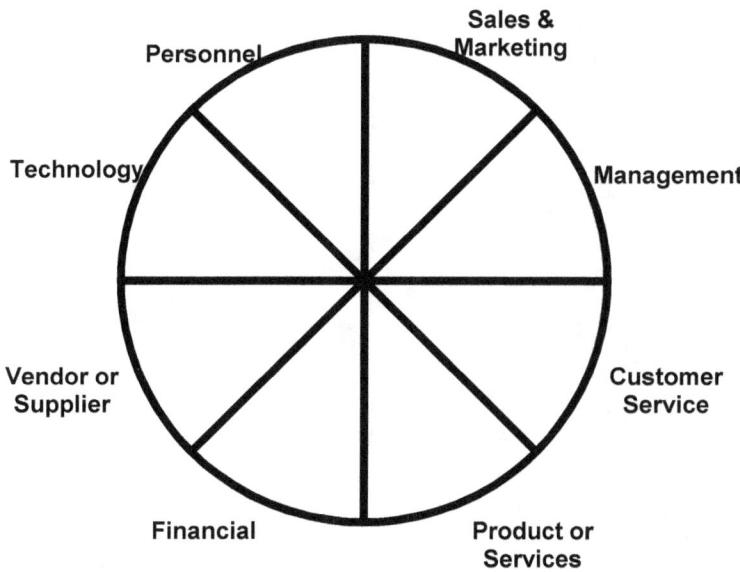

Image #4: Strategic Calendar for Responsibilities and Time Allocation

Responsibility	Current %	Current Days	Next Year %	Next Year Days	Ideal %	Ideal Days
Responsibility 1	10%	2	5%	1	10%	2
Responsibility 2	20%	4	25%	5	10%	2
Responsibility 3	30%	6	20%	4	15%	3
Responsibility 4	25%	5	20%	4	15%	3
Responsibility 5	15%	3	30%	6	50%	10
Totals	100%	20	100%	20	100%	20

Instructions

1. Where do you invest your time currently? Fill in the % of time and calculate the numbers of days per month based on 20 working days per month.
2. How would you like to invest your time next year? Same as above.
3. What is your definition of how you would ideally like to invest your time? Same as above.
4. Plan your calendar accordingly.

Image #5: Options for Freeing Up Time
(To invest in more valuable and/or more enjoyable activities)

Responsibility	Stop Doing	Outsource	Delegate	Automate	Other	Other Other
Responsibility 1						
Responsibility 2						
Responsibility 3						
Responsibility 4						
Responsibility 5						

Instructions

1. Where do you invest your time currently? List them on the left column.
2. What are your options for getting rid of all or some of each responsibility? Fill in the appropriate cells with the name or resource you might be able to leverage.
3. Prioritize the opportunities to work on: Which opportunity would free up the most time?
4. Which opportunity would be the easiest to implement? Make the change happen.

Douglas A. Packard
CEO/Owner – *Doug Packard Consulting*

Doug gained over 20 years of leadership and management experience before establishing his consulting practice. He had success in several positions in the information processing industry including Account Manager, District Manager, Domestic Marketing, International Product Management and Strategic Planning. He was involved in multiple industries, worked with businesses of all sizes, and traveled extensively worldwide.

In 2002, Doug opened his practice and dedicated himself to helping top executives and business owners define and achieve their own version of success and happiness. He organizes and leads peer advisory boards, provides individual coaching, and helps leaders increase the effectiveness of their management teams.

Doug is headquartered in Portland, Maine with his wife Mary and enjoys golfing, skiing, traveling and spending time with their three sons.

He can be reached at Doug@DougPackardConsulting.com.

www.ingramcontent.com/pod-product-compliance
Lightning Source LLC
Chambersburg PA
CBHW070053120426
42742CB00048B/2507